C000136151

A Life Far From Ordinary

My Life With Spirit

Chris Jacobs

A Life Far Fom Ordinary - My Life With Spirit

Chris Jacobs

First Published in Great Britain 2022

Copyright© Chris Jacobs 2022

Printed in the United Kingdom

Dedicated to my Darling Wife

Sarah.

Acknowledgements

My good friend and mentor Glyn Edwards

My Spirit friends who have influenced and inspired me throughout my journey

I am indebted to the following, who gave their time and skills freely to this project.

Written with the assistance of Christine Stewart whose invaluable contribution brought this book to fruition.

Book Cover Design - Sandi Borrillo

The Photography of Mark Hollowell for the cover picture.

Contents

Foreword

Writing this book has done so much for me in the process of healing and reconciliation. Recently talking to my wife Sarah, who has been an influential part of this journey, she commented that I am not now the same closed person she first met. As the writing progressed, she saw a different side of me emerge, the real me, and she likes him. Moreover, so do I.

A Life Far From Ordinary has taken the better part of three years to write, due in no small part because as the book grew, so did I, and I had to revisit it many times. It revealed how dispassionate I had been in disclosing the suffering I lived through. I had closed a large part of who I was. Therefore, I had gone through life's motions and did not permit myself to feel the pain. Thinking now retrospectively, I see how I lived as a shadow. My sister once said, 'I see you existing, but you are not living.' I now understand what she meant.

I have always had one foot in the spirit world and one foot in the physical. I thank God for this. Had it not been the case, I do not believe I would have survived the trauma and rigours of my formative years. I turned my life around, and my message is that you, too, are more powerful than you perhaps perceive. With the Spirit World's love guiding us, I know we all can rise above the most challenging situations. I did, and now in charge of my life, I can enjoy really living. I wouldn't change a thing.

Chris Jacobs 2022

A Life Far From Ordinary

"Everything starts with you and ends with you."

A Life Far From Ordinary

Chapter 1

Let Us Begin

"The promise is kept when the first step is taken."

Every story starts somewhere, and mine began in 1963 when my fifteen-year-old mother became pregnant. The 1960s was a decade of rapid change and social upheaval but outdated Victorian attitudes towards unwed mothers remained. My grandfather, a staunch Catholic from Southern Ireland, regarded pregnancy outside marriage as the ultimate sin. His solution to this problem and to conceal this great shame was to insist my mother be sent to one of Ireland's now-notorious Magdalene laundries. These punitive 'houses of shame' were run by nuns who referred to their charges as "fallen women". Cruelly their babies were taken from them and handed over to wealthy couples in exchange for a handsome "donation" to the convent, while the traumatised mothers laboured for years in what was no better than a prison laundry.

Thankfully my English grandmother wouldn't hear of it. She sought the counsel of the local priest. He informed her that there were other church-run places for unwed mothers around the country where my mother could have her baby. Girls could go there as the pregnancy progressed and have their baby away

1

from prying eyes. These mother and baby hostels were only marginally better than the Magdalene houses, but they were not places of kindness. Hostility towards young women who 'had gotten themselves into trouble' prevailed. My gran found a suitable place in Bristol for my mother, and it was there within a convent that I made my entrance into this world.

My grandfather insisted that marriage was the preferred option for my parents and went to see my father's parents demanding that their son 'do the right thing' and marry immediately after my mother gave birth. Only children themselves and under immense pressure, my parents had little choice other than to comply with their respective families' wishes. Our family life began with us living with my father's parents.

Once my parents were safely married, my maternal grandparents, who never really got over my mother's shameful sin, took a considerable step back, practically disowning their daughter. A situation that wouldn't change throughout my mother's life. Within a year of my birth, they were pregnant with my sister and our growing family moved into a flat in St Anne's. Four children, all girls, followed me in quick succession. By the time my mum was twenty-two, she had five children under seven.

Spirit was with me from my entrance into this world and after that every day since. Please see the photograph (overleaf) which was taken the day after my birth in the convent where I was born. It clearly shows the spiritual presence of a nun. This picture has not been altered in any way.

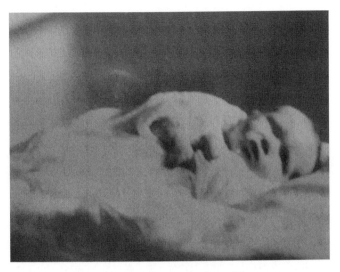

The author at one day old.

Chapter 2

Mother

"The teacher taught, but never understood the lessons."

My earliest recollections of my life were that there were problems from the beginning within our family. I always knew that we were poor, money was scarce, and my clothing reflected this. I was small and malnourished for my age, and I was always hungry. Mother always found solace in alcohol, and this became worse the older I got, playing a big part in my childhood. She never tired of telling me that I was worthless, evident in the way she took all her frustrations out on me. I suffered extensive physical and mental abuse at her hands during my entire childhood.

Physical abuse became a regular part of my life. I became so used to it that I expected it and eventually learned how to block it out with the help of my Spirit friends. The verbal and mental abuse was far worse; it was torture! Being the eldest sibling and the only boy, I felt that it was my place to protect my sisters, and it wasn't unusual for me to submit myself in their place to save them the pain of punishment. Although my father was never abusive physically, he was

4

emotionally remote to me. If he was aware of his wife's cruelty to his children, he never said or did anything to stop it. During this time of great pain and sadness, I became aware of the comfort and love around me from another source and that I wasn't alone and that someone was protecting me.

Painfully shy and without a voice, I became adept at being not seen and not heard. I learnt to walk silently so as not to attract attention to myself. Early in life, I realised that any scrutiny from my mother would never be a positive thing. I kept myself to myself, but I was always keenly aware I wasn't on my own. I was conscious of kindly spirit people who just seemed to be around, and their warm smiles would help me get through my days and nights. They appeared gracious and caring; I would hear their thoughts and see a face smiling at me. These spirit people would alert me to impending physical abuse with a simple "be prepared" whispered in my ear. When I felt so unhappy, I would hide away and cry, wondering what I had done wrong. At these times, they would show themselves so clearly to me that they appeared to be just as solid as you and me. They said nothing, yet I would feel the richness of their love.

One seemed very different to the others. My attempt to describe this being who seemed to radiate light seems inadequate, beyond words even. My young mind perceived this being as an angel. I always felt overwhelming waves of love and compassion emanating from him. It was intense but comforting. Unaware of any specific detail, I always thought of him as male. I now know that this was my guide I was seeing. From him came the unconditional love and strength I needed to carry on. It was commonplace for me to see him and the other spirit people, especially at challenging times. They had been around me for as long as I could remember. It wasn't until I got older that I realised that the people I saw were spirits, and my family was not conscious of them. They never mentioned them, and I was wary of attracting attention from anyone, particularly my mother, so I never spoke about them. My invisible friends were always there when the abuse commenced. I would sense their vital, comforting energy and what felt like a warm, cosy blanket wrapping around me. In a way that I couldn't understand, I just knew their presence softened the blows.

There never seemed to be a reason for my mother mistreating me, but it affected everything I did. Conditioned by the abuse, I was always on high alert, waiting for signs of it happening again. Even when I slept, I never fully rested. I was a light sleeper, waking when someone came into my room. I could tell if it was Spirit; there was a marked difference in the energy. It wasn't threatening, unlike when my mother came in. I regularly wet the bed in a constant state of fear, which remained the case until I left home. That gave my mother another reason to punish me.

I couldn't win. My mother hit me for wetting the bed, and when I was so afraid to tell her that I tried to hide it, she punished me again. My love for her evaporated during a particularly severe beating when I was about nine. Although I do not recall why I was being 'punished', I do remember that it took place on the stairs. After several blows, the final one landed on my face. I remember this so well because, at that moment, my life changed. I felt my heart snap and knew something had left me. Turning to my mother, I said, 'There is no love here for you.' and I knew it, there wasn't. I could see that she knew that too. My spirit friends, who helped soften this cheerless existence, provided the strength that I needed to speak out. They were always there, giving love and comfort that was lacking from my mother. I realised that they also guided me to those kind people in the physical world who would help me.

I formed a friendship with a girl who lived nearby. She was unpopular with the other children, but my friend had the great fortune of having a mother, unlike me, who looked after her and fed her well. I regularly went to her house, primarily knowing that I would get something to eat. Sometimes, I wonder if I took advantage of our friendship, but hungry children rarely consider their motives for obtaining food.

Then there was Alice, a dear lady. Although I did not know her age, she was a kindly lady in her senior years who was severely disabled. She lived in a bungalow just around the corner from me. Living alone, Alice appeared to have no family or friends of her own. I never saw any visitors apart from infrequent visits from carers, and I never saw her go out. I gravitated towards her as I did all older people because they never presented a threat to me. It was something that I couldn't describe then but now recognise that I was drawn to them on a soul level. Realising that Alice couldn't do much for herself, I would do odd jobs for her; this included bringing in the coal from the coal house and setting and lighting her fire. Often, she would say to me to take the 'Slack' home to burn on our fire. It was only coal dust; it didn't burn well and clogged up the chimney. My mother wouldn't use it, and Alice earned the unfortunate name of 'Slack Alice' from my mother.

My memories of this kindly lady were of her long dark hair, which was slightly greasy and hung in what I thought like rats' tails. She had a somewhat dishevelled appearance which kept the locals away, fearing her to be a witch. I even wondered the same thing myself. She had an uncanny ability to correctly call out my name as I walked into her house, although she couldn't possibly have seen me from where she sat in her lounge. It was a relief when I realised witchcraft wasn't at work at all. She had a perfect view of who was coming through the door from where she sat, courtesy of a strategically placed mirror on her wall.

I regularly did other chores for her, and in return, she would give me food, often a yoghurt which was a real luxury to me. She would tell me to help myself from the pantry as I left. I'm ashamed to admit that I occasionally took two, notably when I was famished. Alice never confronted me about this, but I'm sure she would have known why I had taken them. One day whilst I was knelt lighting her fire, I turned and asked her if she ever got lonely. Her answer stumped me.

Looking straight at me, almost as if she was looking into my soul. She said that she had her friends "just like you" and that "you above all will fully understand what I mean by that one day." Although she never said it at the time, I now know that she, too, was a medium. I have never forgotten her words or her face. She will always live on as the beautiful soul that I remember.

My mother had a part-time evening job at a club in the next town, a place called Lytham. My father also worked there part-time as a bar steward several nights a week. Sometimes they would both be on shift simultaneously, and it was then that we children were left in the care of two sisters who were our babysitters. To compound my misery, they began sexually abusing me. I was very young, and as a result, I didn't reveal this to anyone at the time. Not having a safe place or someone I trusted meant telling my parents about this would have been impossible. Mother indeed would not have received such a revelation well if she believed it at all in the first place. My relationship with her meant that she rarely, if ever, listened to anything I said anyway.

When I was ten, my parents' volatile marriage ended. Some months earlier, my mother had met a farm labourer called Ted at the club where she worked. They had an affair, and when my father found out, my parents' marriage disintegrated. Ted lived in a tied cottage on a large farm. After many arguments between my parents, my mother went to live with him taking my sisters with her. There was no feeling of loss from me concerning my mother going. I was glad that she was leaving, and when given a choice of who I wanted to be with, I opted to stay with my father, believing that life would be more straightforward away from the source of my pain. I didn't account for the emotional turmoil I would feel at losing my sisters.

Deeply affected by the split from my mother, my father was distracted and often cried, leaving me very much to my own devices. It appeared that he seemed to be unaware of me most of the time. When I became ill while at the club where he worked, he called a cab, gave the driver the fare and sent me home. Beyond that, there was no further interest in what was wrong. Eventually, he decided that we should move into his parents' home. Both my Nan and Grandad were lovely gentle people. I have warm memories of spending time with my Nan, who was severely disabled. I could have stayed with my father and my grandparents, knowing that there would be no violence, but the concern for my sisters was a constant worry that agonised me. I worried about what was happening to them now that I wasn't there to protect them from my mother's rage. I missed them too. After a few months with my father, I decided to join my sisters and move to the farm to be with them.

On the day of my moving out, my Nan went into hospital to have her pacemaker replaced. Unfortunately, she did not recover from the procedure. Her dying was to weigh heavily on my young mind for some time. She had seen my packed bags by the door and knew I was leaving, and I could see it upset her. For the longest time, I would believe her distress at my going had in some way contributed to her death.

My mother had arranged for a taxi to pick me up from my grandparents' home, but my father came home early and saw my bags and me waiting and insisted he would take me to the farm. During the half-hour car journey, I could sense my father's anger. There was an awkward silence between us that I could feel even at that age. A silence that was only broken when he turned and asked me if I was sure the move was what I wanted. I said that it was. As I was to learn much later in life, he never considered that it was my sisters that I wanted to be with. He believed I had rejected him and chosen my mother over him. His displeasure towards me was further displayed when he stopped the car a few hundred yards from our destination and childishly informed me that he would now send back the new (badly needed) jacket he had bought for me. The realisation dawned on me how immature he was, and I recall thinking, "My God! I don't have any parents." From that point on, I never really had a relationship with my father. Only in the latter few years of his life did he reveal that he thought I had always hated him. I had responded, 'Dad, how could I hate you? I didn't know you.' There was no answer from him, only silent tears.

Chapter 3

Brief Happiness

"Happiness is not an illusion when it is lived"

Preese Hall Farm stood perched among trees on a small hill surrounded by rolling fields. Only accessible via the Ministry of Defence Road that ran through Weeton Army Barracks, the home of the 1st Battalion, the Lancashire Fusiliers. Father drove alongside the high-security fencing to our left, where the base was situated. We passed the married quarters for service personnel and a small wooden school to our right. The approach was beautiful. As the fencing disappeared, the road began to incline through fields and trees, hiding the farm from view. At the top of the hill, I saw for the first time the place that would feature in some of my happiest memories, and it was here that my father stopped the car. Without a word, I got out of the car and grabbed the two bin liners containing all my worldly possessions. I shut the car door, and my father drove away. There was no goodbye, he stared straight ahead, and I watched him go out of view. I felt some pain, but mostly I felt empty. And then the familiar voice in my mind said,

"It's going to be ok".

I turned and saw my mother walking over the cobbles towards me. I noticed a beautiful copse of trees to my left, and on my right, there were various outbuildings, large barns, and machinery dotted around. Four tied cottages belonging to the farmworkers sat near the distance. Picking up my bags, I walked toward my mother. Again, I felt nothing upon seeing her. I was accepting of the situation. She took me into one of the cottages, my new home, and introduced me to Ted. Ted had his children living with him. His son was similar in age, and his daughter was slightly older than me. My sisters, on hearing my voice ran excitedly into the room, greeting me with hugs and squeals. It was beautiful to see them again. Ted's children and my sisters gave me a tour of the farm. I had never seen such a place.

Fields stretched out as far as the eye could see. There were animals that I was able to get close to and touch. The big hay barns would provide endless fun in the coming days as we jumped and ran over the bales, throwing ourselves from great heights into the soft straw. Living in the barn was a colony of feral cats. Fascinated, I watched them for hours as they darted in and out of the barn, carrying mice in their mouths to the nests they had made in the straw. I had never had so much fun. It was a truly magical place for children, and I have some of my fondest memories of that time. With seven children and two adults in a tiny house, accommodation was tight, and within a couple of weeks, we moved into a larger empty house next door but one.

Within a few weeks, Ted encouraged me to help around the farm, which I readily did, enjoying every moment. My jobs included bringing in the cows from the fields in the summer months for milking. It always amazed me how they knew which milking shed and stall to go to. For the first time, I realised cows had some intelligence. I formed a real attachment to one old cow called Carmen, she was slower than the others, and I would walk with her behind the rest of the herd to her stall, but we never used her milk due to her advanced age. I would feed the newborn calves, and there was one that stood out. He bounced around the pen he was in. I adopted him as my own and called him Zing Zing. I soon learned how to drive the small Massey Ferguson tractor and later would drive it in the fields.

Harvest time came. It was busy, and the farm hired extra help. As young and small as I was, I was expected to do my part, and I relished this. I worked with the son of another farm worker who lived next door and was two years older than I. We became friends. Our job was to stack the hay bales on the trailer, ready to be taken back to the farm. This work was backbreaking and got more demanding the higher the stack grew. After completing one trailer, my new friend and I sat atop the bales on the trailer as the tractor pulled us back to the farm. I recall it was a perfect summer's day. The skies were blue, and the sun was high in the sky. As hot as it was, it was just magical. As we rode the bales aloft down long winding farm lanes, I could survey all around me and admire its beauty. I felt like a king. Sitting blissfully there, I suddenly felt the stack begin to move beneath us. The hay bales started to part and fall on either side of the trailer. As we began to slide down the middle, I remember thinking this was like Moses and the parting of the sea. We hit the bottom of the trailer with a loud thump. Boy, did that hurt! Standing up, we both giggled uncontrollably. It was one of those rare moments in which I laughed freely. A feeling rarely granted me during my childhood.

I also recall looking at my mother during these early days on the farm. She seemed happy—something I had not seen before, and I wondered if she had changed. Perhaps some part of me hoped that her new circumstances had sweetened her temper. Sadly, that hope dissolved when she launched a cup of hot tea at my head not too long after I had moved in.

While Ted was around, she was pleasant and kind to all the children, including me. I got on well with Ted's kids, they were friendly enough, and I never saw my mother being unkind to them. They regularly at the weekend went to their mother, who at that time lived in Manchester. One time as we said goodbye to them, my mother turned to me as they drove away and said, "Right, that's that then, the cuckoos are out of this nest". I didn't understand what she meant then, but we never saw Ted's children again.

It was 1976, and the British Isles sweltered through what was to be the hottest summer for more than 350 years. With this heatwave came a severe drought. Water was rationed, and standpipes in the streets were the order of the day for most British citizens. The farm was happily exempt from this. The long hot days were idyllic for a child living on a farm. There was so much to explore, and I loved the freedom it offered me. I felt like an adventurer exploring the dark recesses of the woods at the bottom of the farm. I never dreamt that I could have so much freedom instead of always being on the alert for my mother's wrath. I made friends with a couple of boys from the army base below the farm. We enjoyed each other's company that summer, running through cornfields we weren't supposed to and fishing in the farm pond. As the heatwave persisted, the pond was in real danger of drying out. I was dismayed to see eels lying, apparently dying, out in the field where the pond was. I was unaware of what they were doing, but instead of putting them back in the nearer pond, I followed what I felt someone was guiding me to do. I ran back to the house, got an old shopping bag, filled it with the stranded eels, and deposited them into the stream at the bottom of the field so they could begin their migration to what I now know are their breeding grounds. As the heat persisted, I would often cool off in the large water tank provided for the cows to drink from. I found it great fun submerging myself in the water below the surface and jumping up to frighten the cows when they came to drink.

I had a natural affinity with animals. On the farm was a gigantic bull called Dew Boy. He was enormous, and I had never seen the like before, weighing in at over a ton. Despite being warned to stay away from him for my own safety, nevertheless, like a moth to a flame, I was uncontrollably drawn to him. I knew that I was safe, so I would go and stroke and talk to him. On one particular day that I remember, my mother walked through the farmyard, and to her horror, she found me asleep in Dew Boy's pen. I was leaning against his massive frame as he lay on a bed of straw, gently chewing hay contently. This tender moment is why I have more trust in animals and nature than I ever did in human behaviour. It was the love and trust that they showed me. To this day that love and trust remain and works both ways.

On another occasion, I rescued a rat from a pit that fed barley into a Silo. No matter how small, all life was meaningful to me, even a rat. This poor creature had fallen in and, unable to scale the vertical walls, faced certain death. The pit was impossibly deep and too dangerous for me to climb into. I found some old twine used to wrap hay bales, and I literally threw the small rodent a lifeline. The rat seized the string in its mouth and forelimbs, and I proceeded to lift it out. As it scuttled away, it stopped, turned, and looked back, twitched its nose before going on. To this day, I will always believe he was thanking me.

I was not used to the availability of food on the farm, to which workers were free to help themselves. There were potatoes, eggs, milk and other seasonal produce. I never knew hunger whilst we lived there. My relationship with Ted wasn't particularly close, but he was good to me, and I liked helping him. He was a tall, pleasant man who genuinely took an interest in me. I don't think the way my mother treated me sat well with him. Not being his son, I believe he felt unable to speak to her about it. One day we were working alone on the farm, and he turned to me and said, 'It's a hard life, isn't it, boy?' I agreed, and Ted said no more.

He suggested that I might like to get a bike for my upcoming 11th birthday. I'd never had a bike before, and Ted acquired one. I had a lot of fun on it until one day something went wrong and my mother took it to a local village shop for repair. For months I asked about my bike. Was it fixed? When could I have it back? The answer was always the same from my mum, 'No'. One day I realised it was no good asking anymore. My bike had been sold.

I speak so warm and fondly of the farm because it was the happiest time of my childhood. Sadly these memories are bittersweet, mixed with the ongoing cruelty from my mother and the sadness I felt at my grandmother's passing. She had died within a few days of my arrival at the farm. I was already aware of this before my mother told me. It was a beautiful still summer night, and there was no wind. My mother uncharacteristically suggested we go for a walk, saying she had something to tell me. We got to the end of the lane where some very tall trees stood, the place where my father had dropped me off on the day of my arrival. I turned to my mother and told her I knew my Nan had passed. At that point, rather spookily, the trees began to rustle in the still night air. And I felt my grandmother's presence, and from my mother's reaction, I knew she had also noticed the atmospheric change around us just as strongly as I did.

It was June, and it was hot, and it was the month for local fetes and fairs. There was a town not too far away from us called Lytham, my family's ancestral home, so I knew all about the upcoming fair, Lytham Club Day. My sisters and I were excited to be going. The day would begin with a procession of differently themed, colourfully decorated floats stretching as far as I could see. Bands played music, people carried banners, and an exciting buzz was in the air. People spilt out of the cafés and pubs that lined the streets. We were in situ in front of a pub, and my mother and Ted were already drinking. I had a growing sense of foreboding watching my mother drink, but we children were anxious to get to the large field where the fairground was waiting for us. The good memories of that day are marred by the terrifying experience we children had on the big wheel, which still haunts me. I could never forgive my mother for how she purposely terrified my sisters and me. As our carriage reached the top, she dangerously started to rock the seat. I could see her laughing at my sister's obvious distress as they tried to grab anything to hang on to. They could have so quickly fallen out. In a blind panic, I tried to hold on to them whilst holding on to the bar of the seat. Health and safety was not as it is now, and this ride was dangerous. I have never been on a big wheel again from that day to this.

After being given a hot dog, we ventured around the

smaller stalls. At a hook-a-duck stall, my mother allowed me to have a go and what a surprise, I won! It was a plastic bow and arrow set, and the bow was taller than I was. Little did I know that this prize would lose all its happy association when it became an instrument of pain. Within a few days, there was an incident on the farm for which my mother wrongly blamed me. I do not recall the incident, but my mother insisted I was responsible and wouldn't listen to my pleas. With her face flushed and eyes full of fire, she grabbed the plastic bow and viciously used it to beat me across my back. The beating was so hard that I lost all feeling after a while. My mother then lined up my sisters and forced me to remove my shirt, now stuck to my back with my blood and showed them what she had done. Their screams, cries, and evident distress were audible, which cut me more profoundly than the physical punishment I had received. I turned and saw their tears and despair, and at that moment, I truly understood what hate was, for I genuinely hated her cruelty.

The next day at school, I refused to get changed for physical education. My teacher insisted, and I dared not go against his wishes. And at that moment, I made a snap decision I would punish him for his insistence and reveal to my fellow pupils a window into my life. With all eyes on me, I turned around and removed my shirt to reveal the extent of my injuries. When they saw the dried blood, bruises and welts on my back, in unison came a loud gasp. The teacher, visibly shaken, ran towards me and began pulling my shirt back on, and without a word being spoken, he escorted me to the school nurse. There was little she could do for me besides bathe my back and tell me to rest. She, too, uttered no words of comfort or asked how I had got into that condition. There was no referral to social services as there would be today. The teachers had repeatedly noticed cuts and bruises before this but had failed to do anything about it. Such was the way it was then.

When times were bad, and frequently they were, I would make myself scarce and travel off over the fields finding peace beside a lovely little stream that cut through the woods. I would sit there for hours. In these moments, I remember letting the tears fall, and I would cry out to God, asking why I was not loved or wanted. There would then come a feeling of peace, like a cloak wrapped around me, and suddenly I would be aware of all the sights and smells of nature, and a sense of safety would descend on me. Even the wild animals would be unafraid of me. As I lay there, I loved listening to the sounds of insects as they busily went about their business. It was so soothing, and nature seemed to want to comfort me. These fleeting moments kept me going, and I never felt alone as I watched the clouds and listened to the breeze rustling in the trees. I felt a profound connection to the peace in nature that eluded me elsewhere.

As far as I was concerned at these times, I was in the presence of God, and I would talk to him. God and spirit answered my plea in a way my young mind did not comprehend at that time.

I knew the farm was old. The land it stood on is mentioned in the Doomsday Book, and records show a farm on the site as far back as 1300. There once were several small monasteries and their daughter houses and even a leper hospital nearby. All were sacked by Henry VIII, eventually falling into ruin. Monasteries were once the hub of rural communities, and at some time in its history, the area would have seen a lot of activity. Activity that could sometimes still be heard on quiet nights.

During this time, I first encountered what people might consider hauntings. I would listen to horses' hooves on the cobbles outside, yet there were no horses on the farm. I heard what sounded like people running past the farmhouse in the small hours and men talking, although I could never understand what they were saying or see them when I looked out the window. I often heard people running up and down the stairs at night, although everyone except me was asleep. I told my mother about this, and she said she had experienced a crying child coming into her room at night. She had told the child to get into bed with her, thinking it was one of my sisters. Realising that the child felt unnaturally cold, she threw back the covers to find nothing.

These events intrigued me. I was never afraid of them. How could I be when I was able to hold a conversation with my Nan only two weeks after her death? I recall lying in bed and clearly hearing her voice. From where I lay, I could see the top half of her in the corner of my room. She spoke to me the way she always had and told me not to worry about anything.

Seeing and hearing her did not seem unnatural, even though I knew she was 'dead'. Ted, who must have overheard me talking when I should have been asleep, came into the room enquiring to whom I was speaking. I don't recall my answer, but I mentioned my Nan. He looked at me, horrified and left quickly. The visit from my Nan was reassuring. The ghostly noises I heard at night were not spirits. They were merely the energetic recording of past events peculiar to the place that had occurred long ago that I could detect thanks to my growing psychic abilities.

Although I never saw him drunk, Ted liked a drink, and he and my mother regularly frequented local pubs. As time passed, their relationship started to show cracks, and arguments between them became our routine. I remember one night they went out, and we children were in bed. I had a vivid dream about a bull charging into my room. It was so striking it frightened me, and I was wide awake instantly with a distinct feeling that someone was warning me that something was wrong. I rushed to my sisters' room to check on them and heard Ted return to the house. I heard him noisily come up the stairs. He went into my room and, not finding me there; he threw open my sister's bedroom door. I sat on the floor between their beds, looking back at him. Peering around the room, he said nothing, and I slept on the hard floor for the remainder of the night.

Mother wasn't with him; she returned the following

morning with a police escort, having received a severe beating from Ted. He was eventually arrested and taken away. Before that night, I had never seen him act violently, but I knew that my mother would have goaded him. She hastily packed and bundled us, children, into her car. I sat in the back and looked out the rear window as we drove away. It was then I saw the little kitten the family had befriended. It must have been under the wheel; my mother had run over it and killed it.

With nowhere to go, social services became involved after we spent a night sleeping in the vehicle. We were temporarily boarded in a local hotel for two weeks, a real adventure for us children. There was no opportunity for our mother to be cruel, so this was a welcome respite. Life was good with warm beds, breakfast before school, and a hearty dinner upon our return. Much to my disappointment, this luxury ended when the council finally gave us a house. It was on a small housing estate in a nearby village. Ted turned up at the new home several times, declaring his undying love for my mother and seeking reconciliation. It wasn't to be, however.

Chapter 4

A Voice in the Dark

"The light will find you even in your darkest hour."

I cherish the memories of the two years I had spent at the farm. It may seem strange because of the pain associated with it, but it was the freedom it had given me that I missed. It will always live on in my memory as some of the better times in my life. Today I walk through the countryside, and the sights and smells of the hay in the fields and the cows grazing take me right back there and make me smile. I remember the happy times of that period of my life.

The new house seemed nice enough. It was on a council housing estate two miles from my school in a rural setting. The neighbours and people I met were friendly. One neighbour had children, and the daughter was to become my first real girlfriend. She was a great source of comfort, particularly when times were rough. I could open up in a small way to her.

My mother continued to drink, which became more excessive, mainly in the evening at home, always after six pm. Money was desperately short, which severely impacted our lives as children. There was never enough food, and the cupboards were always empty, so there was no chance of sneaking extra food. This had a particularly bad consequence for me as I was always at least a stone underweight, resulting in weight and mental health problems around food later on in life. Our clothes reflected our financial status. Although we received a clothing grant for a school uniform from the School Authority, it was woefully inadequate and didn't cover items like pants, vests or socks. My mother would buy these for my sisters, but she never once brought me any. When the opportunity arose, I 'borrowed' some underwear and socks from a friend's house without his knowledge. I'm not proud of taking them now, but I knew what discomfort meant. The child that was me found a way of easing that through my actions. I didn't relish school as I was taunted regularly around my physical appearance and shyness, but I did like going as it offered a free school meal at lunchtime. At least I was assured of one good meal a day. And there was the added bonus: I would be away from my mother's attention for a few hours until the final bell rang when the dread returned.

As her drinking escalated, so did my mother's cruelty. Life mainly consisted of avoiding her wrath at all costs for me. There was still no respite when sleeping as I still had an awareness of anyone entering my room, usually my mother coming to wake me. Drunk, she would drag me out of bed and order me to go and wake our neighbours to ask for cigarettes for her, which was always in the early hours of the morning. I didn't always get a good response from the neighbours, which was to be expected but nevertheless, I could see the pity in their faces as they yielded to my request. I was terrified in the dark streets alone, although I knew the voice was telling me I was safe. Thankfully nothing ever happened.

As she was still in bed, we wouldn't see our mother before school. Breakfast consisted of a slice of toast; if we were lucky, it was usually just a cup of tea. I often arrived at school hungry and tired, looking forward to lunchtime. Our clothes – hand washed as we had no washing machine - by us children on the weekend had to last all week because mother never laundered our clothes. Before going to school, we checked each other to ensure that we looked clean enough and removed any visible dirt with a damp cloth from our uniforms. I only owned two shirts which had to last an entire school year. Before leaving home, we children understood that all had to be left clean, neat, and tidy. Boy, we knew it if it wasn't to our mother's liking when she got up.

My mum decided I needed to get a paper round to help with her financial situation, and she arranged this for me. It was the longest one available and spread over several miles across the countryside. It would take me two and a half hours to complete before I went to school. In the middle of winter, I would leave the house at 5.30am on my sister's Chopper bike. The mornings were black, cold and often frosty, riding a bike with no lights and without adequate clothing and wearing thin plimsolls. I was freezing. The journey of two miles to the newsagents was dangerous without lights as I had to travel along the road because of the lack of footpaths. Come payday; my meagre earnings were handed straight over to mother, and woe betide me if I didn't give her what she expected. The shop owners became troubled by my size and lack of strength, I was very skinny, and they thought I looked malnourished. They knew the round was too much for me, and they decided to let me go. This didn't please my mother, who insisted it was my fault that I no longer had a job, and I was punished for that. I often babysat for people on the estate, the irony being that I was no more than a child myself, and again whatever I earned, my mother took. Sometimes the people I babysat for would give me more than the usual fee. I think they knew that my mother had appropriated all the money.

I would use these extra pennies to buy clothes from the charity shop when I could. This didn't turn out to be a good idea. Knowing they were not part of my wardrobe, my mother spotted these items and challenged me about them. She accused me of stealing them. Not wishing to betray those who had shown me generosity in giving me the extra money, I said nothing to defend myself. I agreed with her that I had stolen them, which led to further punishment.

Despite being what some would consider a somewhat strange little boy at home and in school I nonetheless made two school friends. However, we never became incredibly close due in no small part to my reluctance to let anyone in. I didn't want them to know about my life and what was going on. I thought I was protecting myself.

At home, I preferred my own company, and when alone time was allowed, I made my way to a small group of trees known locally as Quaker Woods. These woods had a reputation for being haunted by witches and ghosts and were avoided by the locals. Within these woods, there were three gravestones. Although this was not a cemetery, it was understood that the graves belonged to a Quaker family hence the name. Unafraid and knowing I would not be disturbed, I would sit amongst the trees silently listening to the birds and insects, which brought me great comfort. I was most disappointed when I found that the woods contained no ghosts or witches. I would have enjoyed having their company. When times were hard, I would make my way to this place and other woods nearby. I could escape what was happening at home and didn't want to be in the company of anyone. These places offered me sanctuary and still do to this day. I would let the natural force of nature and talking to God bring its healing balm. I found the strength and comfort there in the silence that eluded me elsewhere. Although I didn't realise it at the time, my connection with Spirit was powerful, and I would talk as I thought then to God. Soon there would be a distinct change in how I understood God and Spirit that would alter the course of my life.

On the last night of my twelfth year, I was under no illusion that my impending thirteenth birthday would be different from any other day. I was cold and uncomfortable. I was trying to sleep in our small bathroom on a folding bed adjusted to fit over the family bathtub, which hooked underneath the taps.

The whole thing was ill-balanced and often collapsed when I moved or turned over, causing me to fall into the bathtub. Instead of being in my perfectly good bedroom a few metres away, I was there as a punishment for wetting the bed. Deeply unhappy, I pulled the inadequate blanket around myself, and as I lay in the bathroom, my birthday only hours away, I felt desperation and despair. My thoughts were of not wanting to live any longer in what seemed to be a cruel world. Silently sobbing, I got up and opened the tiny window above the bath. The October air was cold and crisp, and brilliant stars lit the black sky. It was eerily beautiful. Feeling utterly alone, unloved, and unwanted, I sent out a silent plea to God. It was simple.

"I don't want to live any longer. I want to come home,"

I didn't quite know where home was, but I knew it was a place where people weren't unkind to each other, and I yearned to be there.

Clear as day, I heard a mature kind voice respond from somewhere in the room.

"Of course, you can come home anytime you want. BUT! Your life has a purpose, and we would like you to fulfil that purpose first. If we promised you that life could be better, could you carry on a little longer? It won't be tomorrow or next week, but it will happen."

I spun around, startled by the voice. As expected, I

saw that I was alone in the room. The voice had come from mid-air! At that time, I did not know that this was a Direct Voice* communication from Spirit. I wasn't afraid, just flabbergasted and strangely calm, then came more questions.

"Why am I here?"

"Why is there no love for me in this life?"

And then the voice again.

"You are loved more than you know."

My questions had been answered, and I could feel that love. It was tangible. I knew a silent pact had been made between us. I looked around the room again; this time, I didn't question anymore. The conversation had ended. Feeling contented and strengthened by his words, I felt this was truly the best birthday I'd had so far. I returned to the bed in the bathtub and fell asleep.

* Direct Voice – This is a rare phenomenon and occurs when a voice can be heard that is entirely independent of a medium and is audible to those present

Chapter 5

Time to Leave

"All paths must be travelled ultimately the timing is yours"

Buoyed by the voice in the bathroom, it instilled in me the confidence that I was not alone in this life that was a place of darkness for me. There was little choice for me being so young but to stay with my mother as there was nowhere else for me to go. Although I now seemed to have gathered strength from that night, the beatings continued but knowing that someone loved me, albeit in the spirit world, gave me the courage to carry on.

The following summer, not unlike Harry Potter, I was confined to the cupboard underneath the stairs as some sort of punishment, my crime I cannot recall. I was only let out to eat and use the toilet. Although I believe the young wizard fared slightly better than I, he at least had a light to see, unlike me, who had nothing other than the light under the door. I never felt alone or unhappy with this situation as my friends in the unseen world were my constant companions. Mother couldn't understand why I didn't appear to suffer as she intended, which seemed to annoy her. My friends encouraged me to make the best of what was available to entertain myself. As my eyes grew accustomed to the dark, I could make out lots of old scrap material heaped in the corner, which I used to sit on as the hard floor was uncomfortable. I thought I could make something from this material, so I decided to make rag dolls for my sisters. They secretly got needles, thread and scissors into my new makeshift home. By the light under the door, I could fashion these dolls for them. They were delighted with my efforts as there were very few toys in the house.

During the frequent beatings, my spirit friends taught me to step aside in my mind, and this helped me be less aware of the physical blows. I was still conscious, however, of what was happening. Little did I know how beneficial this would be in later years of my mediumship.

I recall a terrible beating with a dog leash. This resulted from my mother seeing me plant a potato in the garden. Spirit warned me to be prepared, so I knew a beating was coming, and I began to subdue my conscious mind as they had taught me. As I entered the living room, I saw my mother pick up the dog leash, a chain link, and she walked towards me, swinging it at me. After a couple of blows, I entered what seemed to be a dream-like state as I watched the scene unfold.

I felt the leash impact my head and watched as a spray of blood hit the door to my left. Although I was aware of what was happening, to my young mind, it was like being a bystander watching this happen to someone else. I watched, fixated on the patterns that the blood formed—feeling no pain. When it was over, I was sent to my room. As I passed through the kitchen to get to my room, I picked up a tea towel to stem the blood flow from my head. About twenty minutes later, one of my sisters came in and said mother had asked if I wanted to go and watch the television with her and my sisters. There was no interest if I was ok. It was apparent that my mother viewed the incident as something trivial. I certainly did not want to be near her, so I declined the offer to join them.

At fifteen, I realised I couldn't stay as I feared for my life and mental well-being. The time came for me to leave home just as Spirit had promised two years earlier. For years mother had glibly told me that I was free to leave home anytime. She was now lying on the sofa following what had been the final beating she would ever give me. At that moment, I felt as though life had just stopped. I looked at my mother and into her eyes for the first time in a long time. She knew something had changed from how she looked back at me. She was not a woman that I loved or respected, but, at that moment, I bore her no malice nor hatred. I just knew that there was nothing left for me but to leave. I was like a bystander listening to the words coming from my mouth. From somewhere inside, there came enough strength to confront her. It was as if it wasn't me talking. Someone was guiding me. There was no fear, and the words flowed freely out of me. I believe this was Spirit in action, and my statement was simple.

'You know how you've always said I could leave whenever I want? Well, now is the time. I'm going and won't be coming back,' I announced.

I clearly remember the look of utter disbelief on her face. Thankfully my words seemed to freeze her actions giving me time to flee from the room into my bedroom next door. My only thought was to collect my New Testament Bible. I heard my mother run past the room, believing I had left the house by the back door, allowing me time to escape by the front.

The gravity of my situation now fell on me, but Spirit being ever-present, prompted me to seek suitable shelter. As night fell, I found refuge in a shower room in a toilet block on a static caravan park a few miles away from home. I could at least lock the door and be safe, although uncomfortable lying on the concrete floor. I was hungry and cold, and after a few nights, I knew I needed help. Going home was not an option, and walking the streets armed only with my school copy of the New Testament Bible, which I had grabbed as I left, undoubtedly wasn't a life plan. Making my way to the only place I knew that might help me, I presented myself at the Department of Social Services, informing them that I had left home and did not intend to return.

Social services were thoroughly acquainted with my family already. The lady sitting behind a desk in the office recognised me and smiled. I recognised her as our social worker and returned her smile. My mother had called them to say that I had run away, and the social worker had informed the police because I was underage. I was taken to the police station and questioned why I had run away from home. I refused to reveal anything except to say that I would never tell them what had happened, but I would never go back. The kindly policeman smiled, nodded, and locked the cell door behind him as he left. On hearing the lock turning, I wondered why he was locking me in. I would never run from there. To me, it was a place of safety. I do not doubt that the social worker behind the desk had already filled them in about the family history, and there was no pressure put on me to return home.

After a couple of hours, the social worker picked me up from the police station and informed me that she had found a place in a small boy's home for me to stay in. It was in Blackpool, far away from mother. As we arrived at the house, a lovely lady was waiting who greeted us. She asked me to address her as 'Aunty Betty'. We said goodbye to the social worker, and Aunty Betty showed me the room I would be sleeping in with three other boys. I only had the clothes I had left home wearing, which were dirty and in rags. Auntie Betty, who was in charge of the home, eyed me up and down and asked if I had any more clothes or if there were any to follow. Ashamedly I said no, she took me to a room filled with clothing shelves. I was given everything a boy my age needed and much more. My arms were so full I couldn't hold it all. It was overwhelming. I had never had so many things and asked her if they were mine to keep.

'Yes', came the kindly answer. She put her arms out as if to hug me, and I jumped away in panic.

At that moment, I heard the voice that had guided me for so long say 'You are safe now, just as we promised you.'

Overcome with emotion, I looked up at her and began to cry. She looked alarmed at my tears as if she had done something to upset me, not realising that my tears were out of relief.

Back in the bedroom, I unfolded all the garments looking at everything. I tried some on and selected what I wanted to wear. I pulled on a pair of blue jeans, a blue cable knit jumper, and new underwear! Again, I was overcome, never had I so much choice and my own underwear and socks. Carefully, I neatly folded the rest and put them in the wardrobe. Now I truly felt safe, and from that night onward, I would never wet the bed again.

For the next year, I happily resided in the boy's home, which was run by Aunty Betty and her husband. The home was a large detached property surrounded by a white fence that housed boys aged twelve to sixteen. We all had different reasons for being there. From that first day, there was enough food and as much as I wanted. I put on weight and began to grow. It was a warm and comfortable place. Above all, it was safe. I eventually moved out of the shared bedroom into my very own room, allowing me to study as I continued my last year of education. We boys had the opportunity to do crafting and were encouraged to make soft toys which we sold to fund trips and holidays. This was new to me, never having had a holiday before. The doll-making skills I had acquired during my time underneath the stairs now served me well. I completed my education, and when I was sixteen, I left school and found a job.

Social Services deemed that it was safe for me to live by myself, and I found a bedsit in a house run by an elderly lady who would look out for me. My chosen profession was cheffing at a bar-restaurant in a village outside Blackpool. Having experienced hunger in my early years, ensuring that would never happen again made sense. Working long hours and split shifts as the industry demanded, I enrolled in catering college to gain the skills and qualifications needed to further my career. Deep down, I always knew it wasn't for me, drifting into it only because it served a purpose, financial independence and access to food.

Acutely shy, I would avoid getting on the bus to work if more than eight or nine people were on it. I would rather walk the six or seven miles to get there. I also grew my hair long so that I could hide behind it. Over time I began to trust my work colleagues but never really opened up to them. Now and again, I would hear the voice telling me I was safe. The sexual abuse and my mother's physical and emotional abuse made me understandably nervous and distrustful around people. I did not seek the company of my peers like many young men my age. Being excruciatingly shy, I avoided clubs, pubs, and the young's usual haunts. I was and still am more comfortable with older people.

I had reached a safe harbour on my journey. Strength and guidance from the Spirit world helped me get this far. Destiny had a path for me that would soon begin opening, but I was content to drift until Spirit would intervene.

Chapter 6

Spirit Revealed

"I will guide you if you first open your eyes"

Get off! It's your stop!' There was an urgency to the voice. My eyes shot open. The rhythmic motion of the vehicle was hypnotic. I had drifted off in a trance-like state on the top deck of the double-decker bus en route to Blackpool's main terminus.

'Get off!' The voice was insistent.

Without hesitation, I stumbled downstairs as the bus stopped. I fell onto the pavement, trying to bring myself back to full awareness. As the bus pulled away, I realised that this wasn't my stop, and I had gotten off a couple of stops too early.

Then I heard the voice say,

'Look up.'

I glanced up through bleary eyes, realising I was outside an old red brick building with gothic arched windows. I noticed a sign that told me I was standing in front of Blackpool Spiritualist Church. Although I was familiar with Blackpool, I had never seen this building before; it was in an area of hotels and guest houses that I didn't know. Being an unsophisticated youngster, I had no idea what a Spiritualist church was. Again, the voice spoke to me.

'Go inside.'

As I looked, I noticed steps leading up to a pair of impressive wooden doors and saw they were padlocked, making any entrance impossible.

'I can't get in,' I told the voice.

 The voice responded.

'Look to the left; steps are leading down to a door at the bottom, which you will find is open,'

Moving forward and looking to the left as instructed, I saw the steps leading downwards at the side. Following the instructions, I had been given, perhaps a little naively, I made my way down the stone steps, not questioning what I might find behind the door. Somewhat reluctantly, I turned the handle to find it was indeed open. Opening the door, a little wider and peering inside, I saw that a meeting was in progress. A glance around the room showed me that the place was full of seated people. This sight filled me with terror. But as I looked to the front of the room, I caught the eye of a glamourous white-haired lady who appeared to be in her late sixties and was addressing the assembled congregation. Under any normal circumstances, I would have turned and run. The thought of walking into a roomful of strangers terrified me. I now know the reason for finding the church was no happy accident, and I would say planned by the unseen world. It was a Wednesday afternoon around 2.15 pm. The voice had led me to this small room in Blackpool, and my life was about to change dramatically. This fascinating lady at the front noticed me and stopped talking. She beckoned to me with a broad smile as if she knew me.

'Ah,' she exclaimed loudly, 'I've been expecting you.' Pointing to an empty chair at the back of the room. 'Sit down, she said, 'and we will have a chat when the service is over.' I later found out that the lady was called Billie and that she was a medium.

Somewhat taken aback by the situation I had found myself in, I obliged and followed her instructions. I looked around the room, happy to go and sit where I thought nobody could see me. It was the first time I had witnessed such an event. As the service continued, I noticed that the people were comforted and enjoyed what she had to say to them.

However, I found this all a little strange. I was wondering where she was getting all this information. I discovered that I, too, enjoyed the warm, friendly atmosphere.

I did not understand what was going on. Nevertheless, I found myself interested in the proceedings. For the first time in this kind of situation, I felt totally at ease. Never once did it occur to me that I would be working on a platform as a medium one day. I had no realisation of how vital this kind of church would become to me. I had visited many churches of different denominations throughout my young life, finding them a source of comfort, but even then, I realised that God was not present in these places but in you and me. I later found out the church I was now sitting in had been influential in Spiritualism's history in the UK. Founded by Emma Hardinge Britten, 'The mother of Modern Spiritualism' in 1896, it was one of the first Spiritualist churches ever built in England.

Blackpool Spiritualist Church

Faithful to her word, the medium took me into a small room off the main hall when the service ended. I was to learn that this was where the mediums sat ahead of demonstrations. Unbeknown to me, I would sit in many such rooms before services in the years to come. Over a cup of tea, we chatted. Billie asked me about myself. I explained how I seemed to have been guided there by the voice that spoke to me. Billie did not appear in the least bit surprised at my claim and carried on talking. I was surprised by what she said next.

'I know that you don't know about Spiritualism, but you understand the nature of Spirit, and my dear, you are a born medium, and you will one day work for the Spirit world.'

Of course, this was news to me! There was awareness of what I now know to be Spirit throughout my life, including my gentleman of light. I never fully realised what it all meant and just accepted it as a natural part of my life. Therefore, I did not question who or what they might be. They were just there.

This revelation overwhelmed me somewhat, and Billie told me what a medium was. She informed me that the voice that had been talking to me all my life and who I had assumed to be God was my spirit guide. Billie explained who spirits are and that some gifted people can naturally communicate with them. She informed me the purpose of a medium's gift is to prove that life is continuous after physical death by providing irrefutable evidence and facts from a communicator to a recipient sitting in the audience who would be able to recognise it as their loved one. Therefore, bringing healing and comfort to the bereaved. After our chat had finished, Billie introduced me to the church president. I don't mind admitting that this rather brusque lady scared me a little, well, a lot. Her name was Betty Wakeling, who I later found out was a kind and generous soul who had a wealth of knowledge of all things spiritual. She was a staunch advocate for Spirit and was an excellent trance medium. As I approached this formidable lady, she raised an eyebrow and looked me up and down. I felt like she was looking directly into my soul. Seemingly satisfied with what she saw, she invited me to join the open circle running at the church on Friday evenings.

Wow! Everything seemed to be happening so quickly. I was unaware of what a circle was or what part I was to play in it. I could never have anticipated where this new direction would lead me. I felt at ease with these ladies and knew I could trust them. For probably the first time in my life, I felt a little special knowing someone was interested in me, a feeling absent from my life until now. With questions filling my head, I almost floated home.

Unlike today, I didn't have the advantage of the internet to research answers to questions the afternoon had raised. This was long before the world wide web came into being, and I wondered what Friday night would bring. The chat I had with Billie unquestionably helped me make sense of some of the things that had happened to me throughout my life, and the events that had transpired at the church excited me. I had no idea what was to happen, but a feeling of excitement, of being part of something that

45

wanted me was joyous. Friday evening couldn't come soon enough.

Friday evening arrived, and I presented myself at the church at 7.30 pm sharp. Painfully shy but adept at disappearing into the crowd, I hoped no one would notice me. It was a large circle with upwards of thirty-plus attendees. We started with a prayer and short meditation. I was always a daydreamer, but never having meditated before, the practice seemed to come naturally to me. The purpose of the open circle was for audience members to participate in communication from Spirit. The medium for the night gave a couple of messages to start the evening. After she sat down, I watched in wonder as these seemingly ordinary people were able to stand up and provide a communication warmly received by the recipients.

Before the circle ended, the medium asked if anyone else had anything to give. I realised, dismayed that she was looking at me as she said this. I felt my face start to burn, and I tried to slide down the chair in an attempt to disappear. There was nothing at all that had prepared me for this! To my surprise, I then heard the medium announce to someone they indeed had a message, and she was pointing at me, and a room full of strangers now all had their eyes on me! Acutely embarrassed, my face on fire, I insisted I had nothing to say. Her strong voice maintained that I had and told me to get on my feet. My worst nightmare was unfolding. I had no other choice than to stand up. So much for disappearing into crowds.

I wasn't sensing anything, and at that early stage of my development, I'm not sure I would have recognised it if I had. Not knowing what to say or do, I began to stand, deciding that I would make something up just so that I could sit down again. I settled on this plan and stood up. As I glanced around the room, my eyes fell on a lady, and her flaming red hair stood out like glowing hot coals. The sight of her hair attracted me to her, and I thought, 'She'll do.' The 'message,' which I believed was a story I was making up, came from random 'ideas' popping into my mind. As far as I was concerned, I was talking rubbish about a lady in a uniform who would have worked as a matron in a hospital. No one was more shocked than I when the lady accepted the evidence I gave. Eventually, and to my great relief, I was allowed to sit down.

After the circle ended, the attendees stood around talking, drinking cups of tea, and eating biscuits. At the back of the room, where I was still attempting to hide, I saw the lady I had given the message to make her way toward me. She introduced herself, and we chatted briefly. She filled me in with some details from the communication I had thought I had made up and went on to say,

'I see your potential, and you are, in fact, a medium, but you need some development; therefore, I suggest we start a circle for you.'

What she suggested blew my mind. Little did I know the impact this was to have on my life. She offered to open up her home to start a circle where I could develop my mediumship. She would find trusted sitters to support me. It would only be years later that I would fully understand the blessing that she afforded me that day. Of course, eager to learn everything I could about Spiritualism, I happily accepted the proposition. The lady introduced herself as Elsie Richards, and she was to become my circle leader and surrogate mother.

Chapter 7

Elsie

"A mother's love will find you in the most unexpected ways"

Elsie was a striking woman. Tall for a lady, with bright-red hair, sometimes hot-tempered, but with a heart of gold, she was always ready to help those in need. She was a passionate defender of Spiritualism and didn't suffer fools gladly. Like many people who work freely to support their chosen organisation without thought of personal gain, Elsie was such a soul. Intelligent and generous to a fault, she had acquired vast knowledge about Spiritualism through her many years and was happy to impart it to others to encourage and further their development. She lived to serve her beloved Spiritualist church whilst maintaining contact with the Anglican church of her childhood. Elsie was no stranger to heartache, having become a widow early in life and enduring the loss of both her stillborn sons. Her enthusiasm for the subject of life after death inspired me as I watched her labour tirelessly for Spirit. Her passion was physical and trance mediumship. Always proclaiming that she wasn't a medium, our circle members occasionally witnessed her guide overshadow her at church or in the circle. She would speak in a deep male voice that was definitely not hers.

I knew our meeting was no accident. The opportunity undoubtedly created by the Spirit world led me to the church and put me directly in the path of precisely the person I needed at that time. In recalling the conversation in the lonely bathroom with the voice all those years before, it seemed destiny had wanted me to work in some way for the spirit world.

Elsie lived some five miles away from me in Ansdell, a small town between St Anne's, where I lived and Lytham. True to her word, she arranged a circle to sit for my development as promised on our first meeting. We decided that Monday would be circle night, which suited everyone involved.

On that first night, we were to sit. I eagerly made my way to where she lived. I arrived at a large Victorian house in a beautiful area and rang the doorbell. Elsie answered and led me in, directing me upstairs. Noticing my confusion, she explained that the house had been split into two flats, and she was on the top floor. Downstairs lived her disabled sister and her husband. I learned that this was Elsie's ancestral home, and on the passing of her parents, she and her sister decided to change the living arrangements, giving them their separate accommodation. Elsie explained that her sister and husband were devout Christians, and although they knew Elsie's interests lay elsewhere, they did not want to know what went on upstairs at these meetings. Our activities in the upper flat had to be low-key. Elsie's abode had the perfect layout for our circle, which consisted of myself, Elsie, and four other sitters who were lovely unselfish older ladies who came along every week to help my development. Finally, we were joined by her old toy black poodle called Sooty, usually a yappy dog. He was an actual member of the circle. He would quietly sit there as we sat, proving that animals are indeed aware of the spirit world.

I ended up sitting in this circle for many years, and over time, some of the members changed, either becoming too old to attend or passing to the higher side of life. The constants in the circle were Elsie, me and a dear old lady called Minnie, who kept coming up until she passed, aged 94. When two vacancies became available, Elsie phoned me and asked me to meet her at the local supermarket. I followed her instructions without question. Unbeknownst to me, she had been drawn to two of our church members looking for a circle, and Elsie wanted to see if I felt comfortable sitting with them. They had no idea that they were being vetted. It would be up to my reaction to whether Elsie would invite them to join. On meeting them, I instantly felt warmth and was comfortable, so our circle gained two more sitters.

I want to emphasise that it is a misconception that the phenomenon will begin immediately when you start sitting in a home circle; this is rarely the case. It can take many years before the needed harmony, love, and trust are built up in a circle. The commitment to sitting builds the power in which both worlds can work. Spirit later informed us that all those years we sat when seemingly nothing happened were not wasted, as we were unaware of a lot going on. After some time, the spirit world was able to communicate with us through my newly developing trance mediumship which led to phenomena, including moving objects, lights appearing, and occasionally direct voice. Eventually, our small group would sit in red light, and I would go into what is known as an altered state (trance). Typically, my guide would communicate with the circle through me whilst I was in this trance. These talks would often be philosophical and about day-to-day events. Usually, they would finish off by inviting questions from the circle members. The circle would be closed with a prayer. I want to mention here that in these early days, as far as I was concerned, it would seem to me that I was talking rubbish during this trance session. I wasn't always concerned about what had been said at that moment, although I would start to recall snippets in the days following.

As I was coming out of trance, Elsie would go into the kitchen and make me a hot milky coffee containing six teaspoons of sugar as instructed by Spirit. Ordinarily, this would have been disgusting to me. I could not have drunk such a thing as I never took sugar in my drinks from being a small child. Many years later, I would find out it was what Spirit had asked Elsie to do because this would rebalance my electrolytes. She had told Spirit that she didn't think this was wise as I would be able to smell and taste it, but they reassured her that I would not notice this until such a time that she deemed it necessary to tell me.

Then there would be the suppers that Elsie provided at the end of the meeting. Ever frugal, her concoctions would consist of foodstuff near their sell-by date or things she could get cheaply. One memorable supper was slow-cooked turkey leg made into a stew containing peanuts she had purchased. It was interesting, bizarre, but tasty. When supper had finished, Elsie would instruct me to read for a circle member as part of my development. I remember one memorable message given to one of the sitters who had given up on ever becoming a grandmother. As part of her message, the recipient's mother in the spirit world told her she would become a grandmother before passing to Spirit. Sometime later, she was blessed with a grandchild two years before she went to the higher side of life. Such is the power of the Spirit world. Like all good teachers, Elsie offered me many spiritual books to read. Not being a great reader due to not having books at home during my childhood, my youthful ego rejected them. Of course, she was right. Now older and wiser, I no longer hold my former point of view. I would now encourage all students of this subject to read what is necessary because all knowledge, whether read or gained by experience, is invaluable.

I have many fond memories of those times, and regardless of how busy my life was, I always made it to circle. Missing it was not an option. Near Elsie's house, there was a railway bridge, and I would meet Minnie as I ran over the bridge. Minnie later confessed that she was impressed with commitment to getting to our meetings even though I would walk five miles to get there. Minnie, a lady of extraordinary perception, understood me, knew my pain and showed me great affection. We would walk and chat the last few hundred yards to our destination. This lady is still a great source of inspiration to me.

Through Elsie, I would meet the people who would help and inspire my spiritual growth. Very much an introvert, I was also very naive and accepted people at face value without question. Elsie recognised my vulnerability, and having her as another mother was a blessing. She would protect, guide and teach me through the rigours of life. She believed greatly in me, even when I was unsure of myself and would question what was happening to me. Self-doubt and feeling worthless were a big part of my life and plagued my spiritual growth in those early years. I always feared that the spiritual connection and communication were just a figment of my imagination. I believe this to be what many good mediums go through when developing their gifts.

A series of events eventually convinced me that I wasn't inventing anything.

I had become involved in my local spiritualist church and became a committee member. I accompanied Elsie to a committee meeting at the president's home one day. I was their youngest member, yet I felt relaxed and happy as I always found it easier to get on with older people. After the meeting had concluded, someone decided a sitting was in order. During this, I slipped into a state of trance. Also present at this meeting was an experienced medium. During the séance, she stood up, walked across the floor, and put her hand on me. Being experienced, she should have known better than to do this because as she touched me, it felt like I had run into a wall, and I came back to full awareness with a gasp. I felt dreadful; every nerve in my body was on fire. I was unsure what was happening to me as I had never experienced anything like this. Elsie, ever vigilant and protective, jumped up and rushed over to me to ensure that I was ok and commenced healing to help me. When a medium is in a trance as I was, they are very vulnerable because they are highly sensitive in this state. Elsie was very annoyed at what had just occurred and chastised the medium for putting me in danger.

It took some twenty minutes for me to return to normality, and when I did, I noticed that my stomach felt sore, and lifting my top, I saw a red mark on my solar plexus. Despite my obvious discomfort, Elsie took this as a positive sign that what I was experiencing was genuine, saying,

'Before tonight, I was ninety-nine per cent sure now I'm a hundred per cent convinced that you are genuine.'

During this learning period, I often heard people talking about their Spirit Guides, seemingly knowing who they were. On listening to these people speak, it appeared to me that all the guides were either native American or Chinese. Somewhat perplexed by this, I frequently asked my guide who he was and his name. The response would come, and I would hear the voice tell me,

'Know me by my presence, not by my name. Any fool can fool you with a name, but no fool can fool you with my presence.'

I was not satisfied with this, and I convinced myself that my guide was a Chinese man called Ching. For years both he and I was happy with this arrangement. In later years, I learned how very wrong I was, and in fact, his name is Matthew, and guess what? - he's not Chinese! I only discovered this when sitting alone and talking to him, as I often did. And it was also confirmed through sittings with reputable mediums. I asked him why he had allowed me to believe he was Chinese. The response came swiftly and moved me to tears when he said,

'Such is my love for you that I was willing to be whatever you needed me to be'.

That was an excellent lesson because it showed me how much the medium's mind could affect communication with the spirit world when we should allow communication to flow freely in its purest form.

Through my relationship with Elsie, which continued to grow stronger, I learned about some of the best-known names in mediumship, Including the esteemed Gordon Higginson. He had done many demonstrations and workshops; Elsie had seen him at

Stansted Hall and other venues and knew him well. Through her, he would eventually guide me in my development.

Elsie also sat in a physical circle in Preston, a town some ten miles away, and it was in this circle that she was the recipient of an apport[1] and witnessed asports. The medium would go into a deep trance where physical manifestations would appear, and Spirit would make themselves known. For some years, whilst sitting in this circle, she received a set of beautiful black rosary beads. Each circle member would receive an apport, including Elsie. Spirit would ask her to put her hands in front of her to accept the rosary beads. At the end of the circle, the spirit communicator would ask Elsie to return the rosary beads, which she did. On one occasion, she felt slightly aggrieved as other circle members got to keep their apports. She could not understand why she had to return hers. The spirit guide answered that these beads belonged to an elderly nun who had not yet passed to the higher side of life. This situation continued for a couple of years, and finally, at one memorable circle meeting, having received the beads, as usual, she went to hand them back at the end of the meeting, but this time Spirit told her that they were now hers to keep. The person they had belonged to had crossed to the Spirit world and was happy for her to retain them.

Occasionally, Elsie generously extended her hospitality to visiting mediums, allowing a select few to witness rare Spirit gifts. I first encountered Stewart

Alexander's rare form of mediumship at Elsie's flat. There were about ten of us sitting in the sitting room in semi-darkness. The energy in the room was tangible, and I was excited about the evening's upcoming event. Unsure of what would happen, I asked Elsie a couple of days beforehand what the proceedings were, not knowing what to expect; she assured me that I wouldn't be disappointed with what I was about to see.

Stewart Alexander is an outstanding medium and an excellent representative in this discipline. Elsie was to regale me with tales of the astonishing phenomena she witnessed by him. He is acknowledged now as one of England's best-known physical mediums. Additionally, he was the President and Archive Officer of the 'The Noah's Ark Society[(2)], to which Elsie subscribed. Fortunately, Stewart recorded many people's experiences with outstanding mediums on tape, and Elsie was one of them. Had he not taken it upon himself to keep these valuable records, they would have disappeared.

All the sitters witnessed Stewart enter a trance, and his Guide Walter Stinson[(3)], came forth. Walter was a politely spoken Canadian gentleman who brought evidence of life eternal. He proved this by talking openly with the sitters, whom he called by name, about their daily lives and loved ones in Spirit. To my young eyes, this was amazing! I was fascinated with the voice and intonations of this Spirit. They were very different from Stewart's distinctive Yorkshire accent and local dialect, but while Walter was talking, his voice never changed from the Canadian phrasing, statements, and pronunciation. I watched intently and listened closely, aware that I was experiencing something special.

Even then, physical and trance mediumship was on the decline. Elsie had told me it took dedication over many years to develop, and Stewart's mediumship was no exception; therefore, very few of these mediums existed.

Afterwards, Stewart took the time to chat with us all. I was impressed with his humility, knowledge and how very down-to-earth and friendly he was. I have seen him speak several times after that initial demonstration, and he remains, until this day, a riveting orator.

Still dubious about my ability, I needed proof that my mediumship was genuine.

Elsie was fond of saying, 'Test ye the spirit'. If logical solutions couldn't explain phenomena, we could accept unseen forces were at work. Just such an opportunity arose one night at our circle. As the evening began, we said our opening prayers and sang a couple of hymns to get the evening underway. At some point, a sign would be given to the circle members, which I was unaware of, signalling my move into the altered state.

As the evening commenced and I had gone into a trance, my guide talking through me would start the proceedings by welcoming the circle members and addressing Elsie by her Spirit name, 'Service', given to her whilst in another circle.

'Service! We love your mantra of test ye the Spirit, would now be a good time to do that?'

Elsie readily accepted the challenge. The communicator told Elsie that he knew she had been a nurse in her professional life and would like to utilise her knowledge in this test.

'If you could take the boy's pulse, and we were to stop it, would that be proof enough for you?'

Elsie, somewhat alarmed, replied, 'yes'! But she also voiced her concerns that this could be very dangerous.

The spirit communicator then asked her if she thought it might be possible for me to stop my pulse willingly. To which she replied emphatically,

'No!'

The guide responded with,

'Will you accept this challenge as an experiment?'

Elsie somewhat cautiously agreed to do so.

Usually, Elsie sat to my left at all our circle meetings, and this night was no exception. She was instructed to take my wrist and find my pulse and was asked if she could feel it. She answered that she could feel it, and it was what she would expect for someone being in a resting state. The communicator continued,

'We are now going to slow his pulse.'

Elsie quickly responded,

'No, that is not what is happening. It has speeded up.'

To which the guide replied somewhat amusingly.

'Test ye the sitter! Thank you for being truthful. We knew you wouldn't just say it was slowing if it wasn't.'

Elsie, somewhat astonished, reported that the pulse was slowing and becoming rather faint. Then with an audible gasp, she exclaimed,

'Oh my God, there is no pulse! My instincts as a nurse are telling me that this boy should be dead, yet you are still communicating from his lips.'

Minnie began to panic a bit, saying that they needed to get me back to the land of the living, fearing the worst that I was now actually dead; she repeatedly stated,

'How are we going to explain this?'

Talking through me, Spirit was quick to reassure everyone that they were controlling the situation and I was safe. They said they would slowly bring my pulse back to a regular rate.

Elsie, who had not let go of my wrist throughout the proceedings, confirmed that she was now feeling the pulse becoming more robust. This experiment lasted no more than a few minutes, and there were no lasting problems.

When the circle had finished, the members were concerned that I was ok. Elsie busied herself, insisting on taking my temperature and pulse. She assured the other members that I was fine, and they could not wait to tell me every detail of the night's proceedings. I was still completely unaware of what had occurred that night and felt nothing. What happened was passed on to me by all present as I sat drinking my hot milky coffee and listening to their comments.

This experiment had shown me the true power of Spirit, and all I was experiencing was their work. Logically, there was no way on earth that I could stop my pulse. Until this day, I don't know if it is even possible. I had no option but to believe in and trust myself and, more importantly, the spirit world. Yet it would still take time to become my reality. The conclusive proof was to come later via another route which was so profound that it completely eradicated the doubts I had.

(1) Apport – apports are brought into a physical circle from another location and given to a member. These 'gifts' can be anything from a flower to a piece of jewellery. Asport – phenomena of the vanishing or removal of objects (by a spirit) and their reappearance in another location - Collins Dictionary

(2) Noah's Ark Society was formed to research and investigate everything connected with Spirit.

(3) Walter Stinson was Canadian by birth and is the brother of the famous Boston (USA) Physical Medium from the 1920s and 30's known as Margery.

Elsie

Chapter 8

A Mentor Arrives

"Friendships live forever in a heart of love"

U nder Elsie's guidance, I had become a member of St Anne's Church for Spiritualist National Union (SNU). I was later invited to join the committee, thus becoming the youngest member. They thought my youthful influence might bring fresh ideas and attract younger people to our congregation. As one of those new ideas, the committee decided to host a spiritual residential weekend. I was very excited by this, having discussed which top mediums we hoped to attract. I knew it would be a lot of work, but being youthful, I was unfazed by this prospect. After a lot of unforeseen hard work, a year later, the weekend finally arrived, and the Glendower Hotel in St Annes hosted the occasion. Some of The mediums we booked were at the top of their field, including Gordon Higginson, Glyn Edwards and Ron Baker, to name a few. Little did I know that this would be the forerunner to subsequent years at the Lindum Hotel, St Annes. At that time, nothing else existed apart from the courses at Arthur Findlay College, a four-hour journey south that many people couldn't hope to access. I'm pleased to say the whole weekend was a roaring success.

I had anticipated being able to relax and enjoy all the lectures; however, I was swamped with work, oh the folly of youth! But I got to sit in on a beautiful address by Ron Baker. His extensive knowledge of Spirit kept me riveted to my seat. The atmosphere in the hotel was electric, as invariably these kinds of events tend to be, due to the gathering of like-minded souls, all set on a common goal that lifts the vibration.

Later, still full of excitement, I made my way to another demonstration that was due to take place. As I sat there, a larger-than-life character stepped onto the platform, and he appeared to own the room. This man was the opposite of me. He was loud and undoubtedly full of character, and I did enjoy the demonstration and lecture he gave. I was stunned at the accuracy of the evidence he presented. He talked as though he knew these spirit people personally. He gave their names and their careers and described their personality traits. This man was Glyn Edwards, who was to become my lifelong friend and mentor.

After watching the demonstration, I was on such a high that I felt like I was walking on air. I mentioned this to our church President, Dorothy. She informed me there was one medium working that evening that she promised would be both 'captivating and exhilarating.' I badgered her for more information on the mystery speaker, but she remained tight-lipped as we made our way to the dining room for our evening meal. Sitting at our table were a couple of mediums, including the man I had just watched. Dorothy formerly introduced me to him, and Glyn gave me an enthusiastic smile. He greeted me warmly, and we started chatting like long-lost friends. I knew that I liked him straight away, and he seemed to take a shine to me. As dinner proceeded, he began telling me things about my mediumship and details from my life that no one but me knew. I couldn't have imagined then just what close friends we would become.

After we had eaten, everybody went to their rooms to freshen up in preparation for that evening's demonstration. Being so young, this was entirely new for me. I assumed what was to follow was a grand event, so I prepared myself. Thinking that my world could not get any better, I followed the people making their way to the main hall. The room was packed; unable to get a seat, many people stood around the edge of the room. I had never seen the likes of this before. I realised that whoever we were gathering to watch must be somebody held in high regard. I got to the seat Dorothy had saved for me next to her. The chairperson got up and opened the evening; she seemed excited as she introduced 'The great Gordon Higginson' to the platform. An immaculately dressed gentleman of average height with white hair took his place in front of us. As I gazed up at this man, there seemed to be a light that emanated from him. I now know this was his auric field that I saw, and I instinctively knew that this was a very spiritual person. There seemed to be a certain magnetism about him that I could not look away from, even if I had wanted to.

The room fell silent when he started to speak, and the

audience hung on to his every word. His command of the English language was superb and captivated me, and I don't believe I've ever heard a better orator. He spoke for an hour and a half, yet it only felt like moments as my awe and wonderment rose until I felt as if my head would explode with excitement. He delivered some messages, and the accuracy of the evidence he gave was outstanding. My mouth fell open as he quickly gave street names, actual addresses, names including middle names and even telephone numbers to the respective recipients. I and the rest of the audience celebrated with those fortunate enough to get a message from him. He managed to take us on a journey with him, and the message he gave came from a place of love and joy and spoke to us all on a spiritual level. In the end, Dorothy looked at me and said,

'Well?'

All I could manage in response was,

'Wow!'

After seeing Glyn's demonstration in the afternoon, I did not believe I could feel any higher, but when I left that room after seeing Gordon, I felt like I was floating on a cloud. At that time, I did not realise Gordon Higginson's importance to the Spiritualist movement, but I knew then that I wanted to be a medium who worked to the highest standard that Gordon had inspired in me.

Later I sat in the bar having a drink with the committee. Glyn and Gordon joined us, and I was formerly introduced to Gordon. He smiled and winked at me. I was so shy I couldn't speak, so I bathed in the momentary experience I had whilst laughing at his great sense of humour. He became influential in my development through Elsie, and I met him many more times over the years. Like many a young man of that time, my hair always had to be perfect, and he would greet me by messing it up, knowing it would annoy me.

My friendship with Glyn blossomed after the event. He would invite me to various events, which I was happy to attend. Glyn worked as a medium for over 40 years. Internationally regarded as a great medium, teacher, and Spirit champion, he taught me how to meditate, and I learned much about mediumship by watching him work. I was privileged to meet other mediums held in high regard, all thanks to Glyn. Watching these mediums work instilled a standard of excellence I wished to maintain from that young age. In a way, he took me under his wing and was like an older brother, and I was in awe of him. He was also a skilled hairdresser. I remember one time he was going to host a workshop which he invited me to attend and stay with him for a few days. The day before the event, I joined him at his little salon in Southport, watching him work his magic on the ladies' hair.

We often went on trips out whilst I was at his home, and one of these took us to Liverpool, where we visited both cathedrals. I was happy with this as I have always had a fondness for churches, finding solace just sitting in them. I never looked for God in these places because I believe that a part of God resided in me. I was happy to learn that Glyn also shared this belief. He informed me that he had been part of a Benedictine monastery for a couple of years in his early days. While in one of these cathedrals, Glyn wanted to sit alone to meditate in a side chapel, and I went off to explore. I have learned that although we revere such places as spiritual hubs, they are just places of stone, wood, and metal. True spirituality comes through the communion of people who gather in such places with one common goal.

Every medium will doubt the messages they receive in their development's early days. I was no different. I needed undeniable proof, and as so many times throughout my life, Spirit soon obliged me with all the evidence of their existence that I could ever need. Glyn informed me that he sat in a physical circle and had asked them if I might join them one evening. He happily announced to me that they had extended an invitation, and I was to join them the next time they sat. I accepted the offer, looking for proof for myself and eager to learn everything I could.

The day arrived; we ate an early light lunch, and then mid-afternoon, we undertook a meditation to get us into a calm state of mind. Unbeknown to me, after I had gone into the meditation, a full-on thunderstorm was raging. Yet, I heard nothing until I came back to full awareness an hour later after hearing a snap which turned out to be Glyn putting his watch back on, which he always removed before meditating. Whatever would happen at that upcoming circle, I knew that it promised to be an eventful evening. I felt terrific. Glyn instructed me to remove any jewellery I was wearing, the usual protocol when sitting in a physical circle. Reflective surfaces can burn a medium should they produce ectoplasm, and jewellery could also conceal something that might give rise to questioning the presence of Spirit. Dressed in comfortable, loose-fitting dark clothes, I was ready for whatever lay ahead.

As part of his instructions, Glyn informed me that a man and his wife would attend this circle. The gentleman would fall asleep and was unaware he was the medium, believing he was there to support his wife. I was instructed not to let him know the true nature of his role under any circumstances. And it wasn't until many years later that he learned he was the circle medium.

Upon arrival at the meeting, our host warmly greeted us. The lovely lady who was to become a good friend turned out to be Jean Matheson, Gordon Higginson's secretary. She led us into a room where the other circle members were seated and introduced me to everyone. She also explained what the protocols for the evening were.

At 8.00 pm, we went into a dedicated séance room with a solid round dining table in the centre of the room and chairs positioned around it. I noticed small chimes and bells hanging from the ceiling at irregular heights. Jean said that Spirit used these to signal their arrival and often played tunes on them. A cone (commonly known as a trumpet) was in the middle of the table. It had two bands of fluorescent tape at either end of it. Blackout curtains were drawn across the windows to extinguish any light.

We began by sitting in dim red light, with our hands laid flat on the table. Jean opened the proceedings with a prayer, and then we sang hymns. By the time we had sung the third hymn, the medium's wife had informed us that her husband was now under the influence of Spirit. The chimes began to tinkle, confirming that the medium was now in a trance. Jean bid the spirits welcome. She explained that the bells heralded the start of proceedings. I knew it couldn't be anyone around the table moving them as there was no sound to suggest any movement by my fellow sitters. I started to feel the table moving under my hands. Then a circle member put questions to the communicator, and the responses came via the table. Set out on the table were letters of the alphabet, and the moving table responded by stopping when the appropriate letter was pointed at, thus forming words which would then spell out a message.

The table suddenly came to a halt. As marvellous and fascinating as this had been, I eagerly wanted to experience even more. So, with Elsie's advice to test the spirits ringing in my ears, I mentally sent out a question,

'If what is happening is real and true and I am to be a

medium as foretold, take this table, raise it above my head, and I will never doubt you again. Surely this is not beyond your capabilities?'

It was a big ask and an even bigger table, and if it had risen, I think I would have fainted. But something far better happened almost instantly. Before my silent words finished forming in my head, the table began moving again. It was jumping. The other circle members implored the spirits to slow down as they couldn't keep up with it.

Finally, it stopped. All was quiet. And then the trumpet flew off the table and into the air, visible thanks to the fluorescent tape. I had heard of such wonders happening in circle rooms, and now I saw it myself. I watched in amazement as the trumpet navigated through but ultimately missed all the chimes. Whirling rapidly around the room, it circled at high speed above my head, making a perfect glowing ring, not unlike a halo, and then descending and coming to a stop directly in front of my face. I knew no one was holding the trumpet. If they had been, their hands would be covering some of the fluorescent tapes and would have been visible to me.

I was already in awe and wonder at this display of spirit power, and I certainly wasn't prepared for what came next. I sat with my mouth open and the trumpet only inches from my face floating in mid-air. A feeling of love emanated directly from the trumpet, and I could detect a not unpleasant earthy odour. Then, a remarkably cultured, benign voice was audible to all but directed at me.

'My name is Brother David. My child, we are not here to entertain you but merely to prove our existence. Everything said to you is true or yet to come. Know that we love you.'

'The circle is now closed.'

With that, the trumpet gently, almost featherlike, went down and settled in its original position back on the table.

The room was silent. We said closing prayers. I felt as though I had been struck dumb. Time and life seemed to stop; I could not process what had just happened.

As the lights went on, all eyes were on me. The small, experienced group were just as amazed as I was at what we had just witnessed. They realised they had seen and heard something rare. After all, even in the séance room, it's not every day you get to listen to the supposedly dead speak independently. I remember the other sitters firing questions at me. Glyn was impatient to find out what had happened, but I could not utter a word. To say I was surprised would be an understatement. I believe I managed a few incoherent grunts. Such was my wonderment; it took me over half an hour to pull myself together to tell them about the silent challenge I had sent out.

That was my first experience of physical mediumship, but what an encounter it was. I was now convinced. I was already sitting in a trance circle where we experienced trance via myself with Spirit using my voice. To hear a voice utterly independent of any of us remains incredibly rare. It proved beyond all doubt, not only for me but for the others too. I had lived feeling worthless all my life, yet a voice from the spirit world, in so few words, told me differently.

I'm sure there will be those who doubt this experience's validity. It is not my intention to try to prove that it was real. I know it to be true. I will never forget that voice. The tone, the inflexion, I could hear love. Love that was far more profound than anything I had ever known. It felt like waves caressing me, touching my very soul. I often think back to that evening and still sense their love and warmth. I hope I have done justice in the retelling, but I doubt I have. I recalled the promised changes to my life that Spirit had made me all those years ago in the bathroom. They had certainly delivered. The love I felt then and still do is not mine alone; it is for everyone. Life seems brighter and better when you realise how much you are loved and valued.

Although I would see Glyn from time to time, life took over, I became swamped with work, and our times together grew less, much to my regret, and later I moved to the south of England. Some time passed, and I hadn't seen or heard from him in a couple of years. I had a strong feeling that I needed to get in touch. I did some research and read that he was holding a workshop in Kent, and I felt compelled to go, so I booked up for that weekend unbeknown to him. I arrived early and was greeted by his co-hosts as

Glyn was yet to arrive. He came a little later, and when I saw him enter, I was shocked at how frail he looked, and I realised that he was ill. I understood then why I had felt so compelled to go. When his eyes fell on me, he let out a tearful gasp. He came over to me, and we hugged. Oh! What a beautiful reunion! His old sparkle seemed to return as the weekend progressed, and we spent the time catching up when we could. It is a happy memory for me.

A few weeks later, in May 2015, he was admitted to the hospital. Cancer was taking its toll. I phoned him every other day to see how he was. We chatted and made plans for when he came home. Sadly, that time didn't come to pass. One day when I phoned, his sister was to answer. She told me things had changed, and I knew then that his passing was imminent. The next day, he left this world. His death left a hole in my life. Apart from being a great medium, he was a friend and mentor that gave me the confidence to believe in myself. Today, I treasure my memories of him, and I am privileged to have had him as my friend.

The visit with Glyn to the séance, the extraordinary events that evening that we witnessed, and the earlier incident of my pulse stopping gave me all the proof I had been seeking. I would never again question the existence of the Spirit World. How could I? I knew for sure that the inhabitants of that world were able, given the right conditions, to communicate with people in the physical world to prove life's continuation. I now understood that it wasn't me making things up; Spirit was using me to deliver their message and had given me confirmation of that. It was a lot to take in, but doubt was replaced by the absolute certainty that has remained unequivocal to this day.

Chapter 9

Marie

"Angels come in many shapes"

Although life seemed to be much better, my past experiences still undoubtedly haunted me and thus still had an effect – there were still situations that I could not cope with. Minor incidences could trigger me to hide and try as I thought to protect myself. This time in my life was one of great learning for me. I had never been particularly close or trusting of other people. Spirit had kept me buoyed when I needed the extra support. I was approaching a point where I would need to trust people and form relationships with them to have a full and meaningful life. Elsie, Glyn, and Marie all came into my life in more or less the same time frame, and together they taught me how to believe and trust in people and myself. Earning my own money, I had a lovely home where I felt protected and found new friends within the Spiritualist movement. Life was undoubtedly better, but my childhood meant I had built walls around my emotions and heart. My fear of getting close to someone or allowing them to get close to me scared me so much that I eventually pulled myself away from forming deeper friendships. Marie was to change all this. Like a bulldozer knocking down walls, she broke through mine and revealed emotions

I never knew I had.

I overate and became an unhealthy weight, which seemed to keep people away from me, the desired effect I intended. I hid behind my size while filling the empty void within me by taking on additional seasonal jobs. It wasn't tricky living in a seaside resort to find them, and I became nothing short of a workaholic dividing my time between attending circle, working three jobs, eating and sleeping. There was no room for anything else, and that's how it could stay as far as I was concerned. Unbeknown to me, all of that was about to change.

Fairhaven Lake sits between Lytham and St Anne's on the Fylde coast. It is a saltwater lagoon popular with tourists, and I heard that the café that stood next to the lake was hiring weekend staff. Determined to fill a few unfilled hours, I presented myself at the café to get some extra work. The café with its ice cream parlour on the right-hand side was busy when I walked into it on that first day. I heard a lady shouting orders. Her voice rose above the hustle and bustle of the eatery. I soon realised that this was Marie I had come to see for a job. The prospect of this somewhat terrified me. After what could loosely be called an interview based on little more than how I looked, I was hired on a trial basis, never imagining for a moment that this lady would become hugely significant in my life.

Marie was born in Italy, where she spent her formative years before coming to the UK as a child.

Following a bite from a feral cat whilst on holiday in Italy, she developed Elephantiasis, resulting in her legs becoming huge. Effectively disabled by this, it never stopped her from living life to the full. She was a big lady with an even bigger heart. Marie was a spinster who had no children and lived with her ageing father. Her dark hair and flashing eyes betrayed her Latin heritage. She had a hot temper and would hire and fire on a whim. She met any transgression of her exacting standards with waving arms and a rapid tongue lashing. She ran a very tight ship, and her impeccable standards, which she also expected from her staff, meant she had little or no patience with laziness or incompetence. To some, she may have seemed like a tyrant, but as I was to find out, she reserved an easy laugh and warm smile for those who touched her heart.

I was more than a little scared of her. Initially, I kept to myself. I spoke only when spoken to, hoping I wouldn't attract unwanted attention. I was solely responsible for cleaning tables, clearing rubbish, and washing floors. Marie insisted on using copious amounts of strong bleach and washing up liquid, and the vapours were so intense I would often become lightheaded. She insisted I use so much that I'm still amazed I didn't succumb to the fumes and choke to death. As time passed under her watchful eye that missed nothing, I was allowed to serve customers, cook meals, and make sandwiches to her rigorous specifications.

At lunch one day, Marie invited me to sit with her. She

informed me that despite her initial doubts, I had nevertheless impressed her with my work and clothes. My mother's lack of domestic skills meant we children had been doing our laundry from an early age, and I prided myself in always being well turned out. Clothes shopping was my comfort blanket. I was always buying new things and would never wear the same item twice in the same month, another relic from childhood, and the embarrassment I felt when we had nothing but shabby and ill-fitting apparel. I was happy Marie had noticed my efforts.

My quietness intrigued her, and she seemed to sense I had a story to tell. This became a challenge, and she tried to reveal the real person underneath the façade I presented. I quickly warmed to Marie for someone so shy, and we soon chatted freely. Before long, our conversation turned to spiritual matters. I told her about some of my experiences to date. Like so many people Marie, a devout catholic, oscillated between thinking mediumship was 'cavorting with the devil' (she would cross herself) and being excited and intrigued and wanting to know more about it. She thought it was all a 'bit naughty,' but she enjoyed it anyway and would get very excited about such things.

After working for her for some time, our relationship had grown into more than employer and employee. Marie broke through my defences, and we became close. I continued working for her even though I had no real need to, just because I wanted to be around her.

During this time, I knew she was looking to move, and without any effort from me, I heard myself assuring her that the apartment she was looking to rent in an upmarket part of town would be hers by the end of the month. Intrigued, Marie asked me where I was getting my information, and I confidently told her that her (deceased) mother was there with us and that she had told me it would be so.

Marie naturally wanted to believe this, but the chances of a positive outcome appeared bleak for several reasons. However, within the month, she signed the contract on the apartment just as her mother had predicted.

A few days later, Marie presented me with a bottle of Chanel Antaeus, an expensive aftershave. Unaccustomed to such an extravagant gift, I had difficulty processing her actions. Not used to being given presents, I was confused and suspicious about why she had bought it for me and felt quite overwhelmed by her generous gesture. As a child, gifts had been rare, and my mother swiftly removed any birthday presents or money given to us children for her use. Marie could see my confusion and told me to "get used to it."

We quickly became more like mother and son, and I soon spent more and more time with her. I was able to open up to her in ways previously impossible for me. Marie loved to shop, and she shopped at a level I was not used to or had seen before, and it was certainly one I couldn't sustain on my earnings. She frequented the best stores in town and was always dressed immaculately with beautifully coiffured hair. I had never experienced such generosity in a human being until now. I became used to the more expensive things in life through her, including my first taste of bubbly. Although I personally only had a plastic spoon budget, I lived a champagne lifestyle.

Sometime later, Marie said to me in a challenging way,

'I bet you don't know what is happening around my sister and me.'

I felt the challenge within me, and I answered uncharacteristically,

'Don't pique my interest; you may be sorry,' I answered immediately.
I felt like I was physically pulling the information from her, and it appeared that this was in some way causing her discomfort.

'Stop!' she said

I did, but went on to say,

'You want to open a business, and the business opportunity you seek will happen.'

Marie retorted with a swift 'impossible' and asked me what I knew. Something in me changed. I began speaking with words that seemed to belong to someone else.

'If you think it's impossible, why ask then?' I said.

'Because I need to know,' she replied.

I had no previous knowledge that Marie's sister was anxious to open a business. She wanted to put it in a prominent place next to the car park. It was a prime spot on the promenade with many tourists visiting that area; it promised plenty of footfall. Any chance of obtaining consent to build there was heavily against her as it was currently just dunes. It would be different if someone could prove that a building previously stood there.

I continued.

'You need to look back historically. You will find that a pre-existing structure once stood exactly on the plot you want to put your business on. The original building was small as your building will be, but given time you will be able to expand, and the business will be successful.'

I was aware that the information was coming from Spirit, but I knew nothing of a building being there previously. I had only ever known it as it was that day, and no one else knew it any other way either. I think Marie doubted my words, but a research trip to the council revealed that there had been a building there many years before. Erased over time and buried by the sand, everyone had forgotten about it. Planning permission was sought, granted, and consent to build was given using this information. As predicted, what would become a successful business was erected on that spot. After some time, it expanded as had been foreseen, and I became its manager.

Eventually, I gave up all my other jobs to work full-time for Marie. My time that once seemed so empty was filled now with a beautiful friendship. Generously I was welcomed into her extended family, including at Christmas, and spent most of my spare time when I wasn't at the Spiritualist church or Elsie's at Marie's home. Up until this point, I had never looked forward to Christmas. I hated the way people would use it as an excuse to drink excessively and then get violent with each other. The sadness I sensed from Spirit was that at this time of the year, which should have been a joyous occasion, was marred by the poor behaviour of some people. For now, sitting quietly on Christmas day, safe, welcomed, and well-fed and watching the television with Marie and her father was nothing short of heaven.

Marie and her father were close, and she took care of all his needs. One day she approached me, anxious about his health and wondering what lay ahead. I knew what she was actually asking, when he would pass. As a reputable medium, I do not believe in making forecasts about people's lives, as they can be very hit-and-miss. And I told Marie this. I never said anything but felt my guide come close to me, instantly knowing the answer. Uttering no words, I reached for pen and paper and wrote down April the following year. Placing it into an envelope, I sealed it and gave it to Marie, telling her to keep it secure and unopened. With a confused look but not asking any questions, she placed it in the shop's safe, and after that, neither of us gave it much thought.

Marie came into work a little late one day at the beginning of April the following year and expressed concern about her father. She had got home from work the day before, and he had begun shouting at her. He told her off for leaving the front door open on her way to work. Marie denied this, knowing that she had closed the door properly, but he insisted she had left it open. Marie asked why he thought she had left the door open, to which he responded by saying that a group of people had come into the lounge and spoken to him. Very alarmed, Marie asked him who these people were and whether he knew them, to which he responded, 'of course, I know them,' and said they were close family members and cousins. Marie was shaken as she knew them all to be deceased. I immediately knew what this meant, and I told Marie, 'Oh Marie, you need to go home and be with him and don't leave him' I told her that I would look after the shop. She did as I suggested, and within two weeks, her father made his transition to Spirit. It was the end of April. What I had written had come to pass and was verified when Marie opened the envelope in the safe.

Somehow Marie had recognised the walls I had built around my emotions, and she began dismantling them without me even realising. She seemed to know what I needed and gave willingly of herself. My counsellor and friend always ready to listen attentively and without judgement as I told her everything about my life. One day she presented me with flowers as I stood alone in the ice cream parlour feeling sad, used and utterly miserable. Just because she intuitively felt I needed them. That one act of kindness smashed through the wall I had hidden behind for so long. It was the catalyst that finally allowed me to face the years of pain I had tried so hard to push away. She opened her arms, and I gave in and permitted someone (her) to hold me for the first time in my life, and I let the tears flow.

Angels come in many guises; not all have wings and halos. Mine came with a hot temper, a broad smile, and a huge heart. I was privileged through her generosity to witness what a healthy, loving family looks like. Elsie was my fierce protecting mum, whereas Marie was the mother that wrapped me in love.

Without me realising, Spirit had guided me to Marie and the little cafe on the shore. So many things like love, generosity and fun had been absent from my life, and I needed them to grow emotionally. All mediums need to grow and develop themselves aside from their mediumship, and Marie gave me a safe space to have incredible experiences that would enrich my life. My friendship with this beautiful soul lasted until she crossed to the spirit world as an old lady. The smell of Antaeus cologne still evokes her memory and the love she showed me.

To this day, it remains my favourite, and on special occasions, I wear nothing else.

Marie

Chapter 10

The College

"Places of learning are more than the sum of their books."

Elsie exclaimed with excitement in her voice. "We're off to Arthur Findlay College!" Stansted Hall was the former home of Arthur Findlay, a grand champion of Spiritualism who gifted it to the Spiritualists' National Union on his passing to Spirit in July 1964. Later renamed The Arthur Findlay College, a residential college of learning, enhancement, and training mediums in the art of demonstrating and speaking. To this day, it welcomes the training and research of students worldwide.

Elsie and I, as well as being members of St Anne's Spiritualist church, were also members of Albert Road Blackpool Spiritualist Church. Each year, there was what was known as 'Blackpool Week' at Stansted Hall. All attendees who had booked to go would take part in lectures and learn different aspects of mediumship. I could not contain my excitement. I had listened to many church members frequently talk about their visits to this hallowed place, and I learned that many great mediums regularly tutored there.

Stansted was the Mecca that I just had to visit, and

knowing I was short of cash, Elsie kindly paid for my place, for which I remain ever grateful. My joy was complete when she informed me that the legendary Gordon Higginson would be tutoring our week. I had met him by now, and I never tired of hearing about his fantastic ability like so many others who had seen him demonstrate. I also spoke of him in glowing terms, and I still do because he was something special. I don't think I fully understood just how special he was even then and what a privilege it would be to go under the tutelage of probably the most exceptional medium of the last century. The trip couldn't come soon enough!

The day of our departure finally arrived. Along with the much-feared but respected Betty Wakeling, Elsie and I, plus the other church members, who were primarily all ladies over the age of sixty, met at the front of the church where we boarded the coach for the 250-mile journey south that lay ahead. The excitement was palpable. Not knowing what to expect but filled with a sense of adventure and anticipation, my usual shyness seemed to evaporate. I chatted comfortably with my fellow passengers or listened to music on my portable cassette player through earphones. Betty had informed me in no uncertain terms that we were there to work hard and learn. But all that seemed to have been lost in the thrill of this moment as I excitedly scanned the horizon taking in the passing scenery, eager to catch my first glimpse of our destination.

Several hours and a couple of much-needed toilet

breaks later, the coach turned off the main road, and a shout went up, informing us that we were 'nearly there.' Our approach took us behind Stansted Airport. I could see the planes landing and taking off, adding to my excitement. Craning necks stretched to look out of the windows as we slowly moved through winding country roads passing quaint old buildings and open fields. The buzz of eager voices got even louder, and some passengers began getting their belongings together.

At last, we arrived at the entrance of a big beautiful late Georgian red brick house, Stansted Hall. As I stepped down out of the coach, the magnitude of this magnificent place hit me. I almost expected a Butler to greet us! I was overwhelmed by my first glimpse of this sanctuary of Spiritualism.

As I was queuing outside with my luggage waiting to register and get my allocated accommodation, I stood on well-maintained grounds drinking in the beautiful vista. As I looked around me, I noticed stately gardens and woodlands with lovely old trees. One colossal tree stood in the middle of the grounds, catching my eye. I always have a fondness for trees, but this one felt special to me, seen from where I stood. I would get to know it later in the week. Fascinated by such beautiful surroundings, I watched horses peacefully grazing. I could hardly believe that I had arrived at the place where (according to Betty) all mediums should strive to reach. As I ascended the steps and passed through the large oak door, I was in the reception. In stepping over the threshold, I was aware of the tangible presence of Spirit. It was the start of what promised to be the most exciting week.

Formalities over and clutching the key for my top floor room, I climbed the grandest and most extensive staircase I had ever seen. The ceilings were so high that they almost seemed out of sight, yet I could identify that they were ornate. Halfway up the staircase was a large stained-glass window, which was beautiful. Huge paintings and portraits of people I didn't know lined the walls. They watched me from their lofty position inside their elegant frames as I passed by these sizeable pictures whilst the antique oak balustrade enchanted me. After many wrong turns, I finally found my room. It was very basic, with a bathroom at the end of the corridor. Before meeting my fellow students downstairs for tea in the main lobby area, I quickly unpacked.

Betty made it clear that she expected us to attend every lecture, and the packed timetable showed a busy week ahead. Everyone participated in an introduction to the week and then the joy of joys; our first workshop was with Gordon Higginson in the library.

The students excitedly made their way to the library, and we took our places. We were treated to a fascinating lecture in which Gordon shared his many years of experience with us, gave us helpful hints and advice, and talked about trance mediumship. Elsie was particularly excited about this as her passion had always been physical and trance mediumship. Following that, he gave a small demonstration bringing forth some remarkable evidence. I was particularly interested and excited by this because it showed me how beautiful mediumship could be when proper blending with the spirit world is attained, I was in awe. My heart was pounding in my ears, and I felt energy resonating within me, knowing this was right and true. My guides spoke to me, telling me to listen and understand what was happening. Afterwards, I left that library smiling, feeling like I was walking on air. I turned to Elsie and said,

'For the first time, I feel like I have come home.'

Elsie turned and gave me a knowing smile. And I did feel that way! It was here where I belonged, at the heart of the Spiritualist movement.

Elsie remarked that she could sense lots of energy around me like electricity, and when she touched my hand, a loud crack and a spark signified that this was real and not my imagination. When I gazed upon this man who was a God to many, there was no doubt that he knew and understood things most people did not. On leaving the room, Gordon looked straight at me and winked. I felt like time had stopped. Silently asking my guides if what I was feeling was confirmation, the response was,

'Yes, it is. Listen and learn.'

And that is what I did. Listening intently to conversations, I tried to absorb everything I heard. I wanted to experience everything I could, and there were so many questions to ask, but the week was passing by so quickly, and fate would temporarily stop me in my tracks.

Midweek I awoke slightly unwell. I managed to get through my first lecture but felt progressively worse as the morning went on. Elsie was unwilling for me to miss the following class with Gordon Higginson. She was suspicious that my sickness was a ruse to get me out of the workshop. Unbeknown to me, Gordon would pick a student to demonstrate, and he and Elsie had conspired that it would be me. Listening to the lecture about the demonstrating medium, he pointed at me, smiled, and said as he finished.

'Come and join me, young man.'

I told him I wasn't feeling well, and he responded that if I were indeed in power with Spirit, they would take the sickness away during my demonstration.

He led me onto the platform and indicated that I was to sit. After informing the delegates what his intentions were and that I was up there to work, he told me to get up on my feet. I was beyond terrified. Never one for seeking out this attention, I would have been much happier had the audience been facing the wall. I was crying inside and pleading with Spirit to help me out. Nausea seemed to evaporate, and I felt slightly better, but it wasn't to be my finest hour. I was able to give some evidence before the nervous sweating started. Gordon smiled at me and told me to sit down. I was relieved that my ordeal was over, and I was still feeling queasy but remained seated until the workshop ended.

A dinner bell beckoned us to the dining hall, and I found myself sitting opposite Gordon. Convinced it was my nerves causing me to feel off-colour, Elsie commented that all would be fine now that I had gotten that experience of standing on the rostrum out of the way. Someone placed my dinner in front of me, and I turned to my friend and, through gritted teeth, insisted,

'Elsie, I don't feel well!"

And at that moment, and without warning, I threw up all over my food. My constant attempts to blend into the background once again became publicly unstuck. Elsie went into a panic, seeing that I was ill. Embarrassed and believing I would pass out, I feebly apologised to anyone who would listen. A course tutor took me up to my room and, amidst my apologies, reassured me that I was not alone. There appeared to be a problem with the top floor as a few people had been taken ill. I got into my bed and passed out.

Feeling better by the evening, I could eat and drink a little food kindly brought to me by one of the tutors, Gerard Smith. I met him at our previous weekend in St Annes. Later, I discovered he was a renowned, gifted, and accurate evidential medium. He is a humble man and took the time to chat with me and put me at ease, which enhanced my feelings of being in a beautiful place amongst special people who accepted me.

One afternoon pulled by an urge to be outside and alone, and much to Elsie and Betty's annoyance, I skipped what I felt was an unimportant workshop and took myself off down a lane by the side of the woods. Unsure where I was going, I felt compelled to turn off into a field halfway down the track and discovered a large pond surrounded by trees. The sun broke through the clouds as I sat down, and a beautiful shaft of light descended on the water's surface. It was a special moment, and I felt like something was touching me. My connection with this place was genuine. The fish in the pond came to the surface, and I could see their scaly backs sticking out of the water. Having only recently found out that the voice I heard wasn't God, I wondered where he was. The answer came swiftly.

'He is here. Look around you.'

At that moment, I genuinely believed that the presence of God touched me. Peace, calm, and understanding seemed to vibrate from me and around me. I understood this to be the presence of God in action. I appreciated my place in this, was fully immersed in it and accepted that it wouldn't be the same without me. At that moment, the insight I received taught me far more than a workshop ever could. I lost track of time, entirely at peace. Everything that I could see appeared to have a silver hue around it. As I looked, I knew that what I witnessed was the life force emanating from everything. My skin tingled, and my hair follicles raised. I was physically feeling this. I don't recall thinking about anything other than just being in that moment. That was where I first understood what God in action meant, although I also realised I didn't need to understand it. The soul recognises it. It reminded me of when, as a child, there was a thunderstorm one day, and I snuck off and went to a cornfield; it was a vicious storm, and the sky turned mauve red. Sat in the field, I initially felt vacant and then experienced excitement in me powering up. I questioned the voice, and the response I got was that this is the power of nature. It is destructive and dangerous, and from the destruction comes forth renewal. I understood back then that they were referring to my home situation. The beatings were shaping my life. Rain-soaked, I returned home to be chastised and called a devil's child for wanting to be out in the storm.

The voice jolted me back to the present and said,

'It's time to go back. You don't have to explain this to anyone; it's not for others to understand.'

I got up, made my way back up the lane to the hall, and headed for the tearoom. I spotted Elsie and Betty immediately, and I could tell by their faces that neither was happy with me. Betty threw me one of her looks that could turn anyone to ice, and a distinct chill had replaced Elsie's usual warmth as she asked why I hadn't attended the workshop. For someone who never answered back, I uncharacteristically told her that I didn't need to be there and that I needed to be alone. That didn't go down too well. I knew I was in her bad books and did everything to turn that around. Betty kept giving me glances as though I had let the church down. The other ladies asked if I had enjoyed my trip out and informed me that I hadn't missed much anyway as far as the workshop went.

Within Stansted's extensive formal gardens grows a particular tree. The large tree caught my attention the day I arrived. Affectionately called The Tulip Tree, said by some to have unique healing properties. Like so many before me, my love of trees meant I gravitated toward this one. I spent time sitting under its canopy, enjoying the tranquillity, healing energy, and harmony whilst musing about my future. I didn't want to go back to my everyday life; I wanted to stay right where I was. I believe I would never have left if Stansted had been some monastical place. Of course, I didn't get all the answers to my many questions that week, but I was sure that being a medium was what I was supposed to do and wanted to do with my life.

It was a monumental week. So many things seemed to be coming together or set in motion. On one of the days, we had a trip out to Peterborough. I had never heard of the place and was unaware of its geographical area, and at the time, I couldn't have known that life would move me within a few miles of that city years later. Things felt right, and I knew what had been missing from my life—seeing Gordon Higginson again profoundly impressed me. His influence on our circle and my training would increase from this point. Watching him demonstrate showed me the power of Spirit and how a medium can develop and refine their gifts. His lectures inspired me. Knowledgeable and passionate about Spirit, he emphasised the need for development, ethics, and integrity within mediumship and famously said.

'Before you can touch the Spirit, you must find it within yourself. For all truth, for all knowledge and all love, must be found first within oneself.'

I was determined to find it within me.

N.B Gordon Higginson saved Stansted. He was the longest-serving President of the Spiritualist National Union (SNU) and an excellent medium, teacher, and speaker. He reluctantly took on the role of President in 1970 when the SNU was experiencing severe financial difficulties. Crippling debts were owed on Stansted Hall, which would mean selling the property to pay them. Recognising the seemingly impossible challenge facing him, Gordon initially refused the post of President. Destiny had other plans for him after an encounter with a Spirit visitor caused him to reverse his initial decision.

Gordon had been demonstrating in the South of England and got lost on the journey home. Having realised that the College was nearby, he rang and got a room for the night. Gordon made his way to the library the following day after being told someone was waiting there for him. Upon entering, he encountered a monk complete with habit who insisted that he take the President's position. It became clear that the monk was a spirit messenger when he disappeared from the room despite the door being closed. Having accepted the role, Gordon threw himself entirely into the challenge of saving the College. He did this in many ways, not least by organising the kind of week I was now participating in.

Stansted College

Chapter 11

Cumbria

"God is the current in which all life flows, so drift in His presence."

After Stansted, there was a shift in me. Back at St Anne's in my little flat, I felt sad that it was all over. The high energy from the week had left me exhausted, and I slept a lot for the first few days. I wondered to myself, 'what now?'. Unbeknownst to me, it wasn't the end of anything, merely the beginning of the next chapter in my journey. My ego certainly took over for a little while. I felt unstoppable. So excited was I, there was no control, and given the opportunity, I was giving readings here, there, and everywhere. I was young and believed I knew a lot. Of course, as I soon realised, I had so much to learn, not just about mediumship but also about myself.

I threw myself back into work again. Circle carried on, and at St Anne's church, I began demonstrating on the platform initially at 'fledgeling' evenings. Elsie wanted to test me, and when a visiting medium failed to appear one Wednesday night, I and two other fledgelings found ourselves ushered to the front of the room. There was a tray on which church members had put personal items, and we had to choose an article we felt drawn to and hold the item whilst we described the feelings we were getting. Known as Psychometry, this is of the old school belief and my opinion, too, that new and budding mediums should learn this discipline when starting their development. Drawn to a bunch of keys, I picked them up and looked straight at a man I didn't know in the audience. I described my feelings and the information I was getting from the keys, which the man confirmed were correct. Then I felt a change, and the rest of the congregation faded. I became conscious of a Spirit coming close to me, and I knew it to be his wife. I returned the keys to the tray, and it felt like there was no one else in the room but him. I gave him a message from his wife, which he readily accepted.

On another memorable evening at the church, I was encouraged to take the platform as the expected medium failed to turn up. Partway through my demonstration to the back of the church, I noticed the doors opening and saw a man stepping in. I encouraged him to come in and pointed out the only available chair in the middle of the congregation. The audience turned and gazed in the direction I was looking. They then turned to me and appeared somewhat perplexed, giving me quizzical looks. Nevertheless, the man sat next to a lady, and I continued the demonstration. After we had finished, Elsie and a few others asked me who I had ushered in. As far as they could see, there was no one there! The lady he had sat next to asked me to describe him, which I did. She immediately said

'Oh my God. That's my husband that passed a year ago!'

I want to add that he was like any physical man. I was unaware that he was a Spirit. I still get goosebumps thinking about it.

I made many more trips to study at Arthur Findlay College. I loved everything about the college and visited as often as time and funds would permit. Just being in that place filled me with inspiration. Sadly, it was there that I encountered a less palatable side of some 'spiritual people'. For reasons unknown to me, a couple of people at the college were genuinely nasty to me on several occasions. Confused, I couldn't understand what I had done to attract their displeasure, so I spoke to Glyn about it. He advised that I stay away from the college for a bit. Another lesson learned, not everyone walking a spiritual path is an angel!

Somewhat disillusioned by the lack of spirituality in some people, I grew anxious and wasn't entirely happy. Life had become a little more difficult as I tried to fit everything in, leaving no time. I became a little desperate and had a strong desire to be free. I once again turned to my spirit friends, asking them what was happening to which they answered, 'it is time now to take time for you and experience life's many possibilities for you to find yourself.' I didn't understand what they meant by that. I could step aside during beatings from my mother, and I was also good at stepping aside from my feelings. I would quickly tuck them away when painful things arose so I didn't have to deal with them. I already avoided large crowds where possible, but now I was avoiding contact with anyone I wasn't familiar with. There was a growing urge to be alone.

On a visit to my doctor for something else, he recognised that I needed help and suggested that I had some counselling to try and deal with some of the issues I was experiencing. Taken aback by his suggestion, I reluctantly agreed to give it a go.

The lady I saw was lovely. Unfortunately, the experience for me was dreadful. Feeling exposed, vulnerable and like every spotlight in the world was on me, I just wanted to run. My eyes kept being drawn to the door, which I had identified as my escape route. There seemed like an eternity of silence as I sat there waiting for her to speak. Eventually, she did, urging me to tell her about my life. I was unable to speak. Finally, I started to relate things from my childhood through her open questions. I was unemotional and cold, even as I described some of my stories, and then I realised that she was crying, to my horror.

On seeing her response, I was distraught. Unable to continue, I left the room feeling violated. I would never revisit a counsellor. That is not to say that I don't believe counselling is helpful. I do. At this time, protocols and training in this field were in their infancy, and the counsellor's unprofessionalism wouldn't happen today. I had to find another way to work on myself.

As luck would have it, and I suspect some 'divine intervention,' I met a lad of a similar age, and we quickly became friends. He told me about where he lived in Cumbria and described the majestic mountains, beautiful forests, and lakes. Although this place was only two hours from where I was living, I had never visited the lakes, yet all of a sudden, it felt like home from his description. I now know that this was no happy coincidence and that this place would bring me great healing, so I decided to move. Unusually this prospect did not seem scary, so whatever had conspired, it was meant to be.

Everything fell into place very quickly. An advert for a chef at a hotel in Bassenthwaite seemed to fall into my lap within the week. Hastily I arranged an interview and was offered a job and was to start as soon as possible. Elsie understood why I needed to go. Marie was upset at my leaving, but I would contact them via endless phone calls. The timeless landscapes of the area, with its famous lakes, forests, mountains, and fells, appealed to my love of nature; the more secluded, the better. The job included live-in accommodation, and I started work at the hotel within two weeks.

The beautiful hotel was undoubtedly remote in the spectacular backdrop of the Lake District, and a car was essential to access it. The shift patterns meant early starts and late evenings, and like most service industries, it was hard work, and I eagerly anticipated my days off. I made a couple of friends whilst there. My mediumship halted without a church to attend and away from my circle friends; occasionally, it would surface naturally. I often found that people seemed to gravitate towards me with their problems, and as we were talking, the mediumship side would kick in, and I would give them what they needed to hear.

Being without a car, my friend would come over, and we would take trips out on my days off, taking in the peace, quiet, and beauty, which all positively affected me. We decided to take a trip to Blackpool for a weekend away. While there, we pulled up at traffic lights on the Blackpool promenade. Immediately my attention was drawn to the large delivery lorry in front of us with the tailgate down. It was level with our heads. At that moment, I seemingly moved into an altered state, and it felt almost surreal as everything seemed to move into slow motion. I watched my friend take the car out of gear and put the handbrake on. I heard myself telling him to put the car into first gear because if something crashed into us from behind, the force of the impact would push us into the tailgate of the lorry, and it could potentially be fatal. My friend rolled his eyes, sighed, and muttered something under his breath but put the vehicle into first gear. As he did, we were struck from behind by a car. Our car never moved. My companion looked at me quizzically and said, 'You're a witch!' I had felt the presence of Spirit and was aware of being warned. I knew my Spirit friends had taken control of that situation. I'm forever thankful they did.

After a couple of months of living and working in the

hotel, I wanted a job that wasn't so remote and not as full-on, and with hindsight, it appears Spirit had just the place in mind. A vacancy came to my attention at a hospital further into Cumbria at a place called Dovenby. The shift pattern would be in a three-week rota which suited me better. I applied for the post and was offered the job after a brief interview consisting of a few questions. There was no live-in accommodation at the hospital as there had been at the hotel, so I needed to find somewhere to move into quickly. A friend directed me to a lady who had a guest house, she also had places to rent long term, and a vacancy had come up two days before on one of the long-term lets. I went to view the flat. It was small but suited my needs, and I moved in within a week. Everything seemed to have been put in place to make a move easier. I was where I was supposed to be.

Dovenby Hall, a former country house set on 115 acres, was acquired by the local authorities from Colonel Ballantine-Dykes for use as a mental hospital and those patients with severe learning difficulties in 1930. I realised that Spirit had directed me there for a reason. I listened to the stories the patients had to tell. Some patients seemed to have been there forever. Their only crime was having a child out of wedlock. In the early 20th century, it was common to lock away daughters regarded as 'fallen women. The patients had become so institutionalised that they could never leave. I witnessed the cruelty of society and its consequences. Everyone seemed to shun one poor soul who had spent her formative years locked up in a shed with chickens, unwanted by those who should have loved and cared for her. To my knowledge, they never visited her whilst I was there. My time at Dovenby taught me about people, the good and the wrong, and about hope.

Dovenby was good for me. I enjoyed my time there and stayed for a few years. By now, I had a car, and I loved that I could jump into it and drive out and find solitude in the beautiful countryside. There was no pressure from my family, and the break from Spiritualism was welcome.

I now understood envy was in all sections of society, including the spiritual sphere. Those people knew nothing of my life, and It was certainly nothing to be jealous of. I still had food issues, but I joined a wellness group run by an ex-Special Air Service (SAS) officer who made us run around the lakes and do various exercises. I got very fit and started to look after myself. On a visit to see my sisters, I was surprised when they saw the difference in me, a reaction that boosted my feelings of self-worth, which was much needed.

Still on my own a lot of the time, I relished the solitude. But I enjoyed life and where I was, realising however bad our lives are, there is always someone worse off than ourselves. The patients at Dovenby were at liberty to roam the extensive grounds, and by being with them and talking to them about all their issues, some of which were severe, I believe I was never nearer to Spirit than when I was with them. Listening to their stories was a real education. It occurred to me that perhaps these people are more spiritually evolved than I am. Through their disabilities, they could help us if we chose to notice and listen. I never found them repulsive or shied away from them as others did, and I was quick to defend them when someone was unkind to them. I found simplicity and honesty in them, a rarity in 'normal' society.

I was still in contact with Elsie and Marie, and we spoke regularly on the phone. After a few years, I decided it was time to leave Dovenby. I received lots of healing through contact with nature and the dear people I had encountered, but some of me knew that staying in such a remote place meant running away from life. So, I returned to the Blackpool area and stayed with my sister for a while. Marie was thrilled that I was back and was instrumental in helping me to buy my first home. She insisted I get some stability in my life and offered me a position working for her, which I took in addition to a couple of other cheffing jobs. I found a modest new build in a small hamlet very close to where I had grown up. Marie's natural flair for bartering resulted in the house being mine with £3000 off the asking price.

My own experience taught me that anyone wishing to embark on the mediumship journey also has a life here in the physical. There is a personal responsibility to that life and your own Spirit. I had returned from Stansted all those years before wanting to fully immerse myself in spiritual matters to the exclusions of almost everything else. The more I worked with

Spirit, the more I wanted to be with them. My Spirit team had guided me to the lakes where there wasn't the opportunity to allow Spiritualism to take over, thus abdicating myself from the physical world I was living in. I had been unaware that a big part of developing as a medium was developing myself fully, which is only possible by living life and its experiences. In that place of beauty, where the only distraction was the stunning landscape, I realised the responsibility to live the life given to me. That life included mediumship which could enrich and enhance rather than dominate my life.

There was hope in the souls I met at Dovenby; their Spirit shone through their infirmities. Despite some of their terrible experiences, they could still smile. I would take strength from them, and the lessons I learned there as a new chapter in my life began to play out in front of me.

Chapter 12

Endings and Beginnings

"Life's lessons may be hard but nonetheless have to be learned."

Having moved into my new house, I set about making it my home, settling back into my life. The difference this time was that my experiences in Cumbria had matured me.

I returned to working for Marie part-time and had a full-time cheffing at a pub restaurant. Whilst predominantly working in the kitchen, I also took a strong interest in the pub side of the industry. Working behind the bar in the evenings, I quickly became friends with a young lady called Ann. Never having much confidence around girls due to my early experiences in life, it surprised me when she invited me out for a drink after work. After spending a few short hours together, to my astonishment, we grew close.

We began dating, and we spent more time in each other's company. Eventually, we ended up living together. She was a beautiful girl, intelligent and highly educated, and before long, I realised that she had strong willpower and would be a force to be reckoned with. Although we got on well together, she wasn't the friendliest person to other people. This trait was highlighted when two of my sisters came to visit. She hid her face and virtually ignored them. I realised quickly just how similar in temperament she was to my mother. I was in love, so none of that mattered to me, and we casually talked about getting married. To which she instantly agreed. I found myself going along with the idea like a leaf drifting on a pond—no thought behind it. At this point, I just seemed to go wherever life took me. There were no warning signs to suggest otherwise.

Very early in our relationship, we got pregnant, but sadly the pregnancy caused my wife to become very unwell, and as her condition deteriorated, it became potentially fatal. The baby wasn't thriving, and after consultations with doctors, we made the difficult decision to terminate.

In the meantime, while working behind the bar, the manager saw that I had an aptitude for this type of work and suggested that I would make a good manager running my own establishment. Therefore, he proposed to me that I should commence studying for a Diploma with The British Institute of Innkeeping (BII). I accepted his advice as the events of my life began unfolding before me once again. Once qualified, an opportunity arose through our area manager. He took a keen interest in me and knew I had the qualifications to take up a vacant post for a relief deputy manager in Manchester. It was here that I gained many skills, and yet again, the area manager noticed this and decided to move me to another establishment in Blackburn, which was nearer my home. The person who managed the establishment left with very little notice. I found myself running the venue, which became a real baptism of fire. I became one of the youngest people to hold a licence in the country. After six months, a replacement was found to run the place long term, and my new role was to become a relief manager—a position I enjoyed as it meant moving around the country as needs dictated.

I enjoyed being married. My job meant I spent a lot of time working away, and I looked forward to the times I could spend back home in my surroundings with my wife, where I felt safest. On one of those occasions when I was home, Ann asked if I would read for her. She had always shown an interest in my mediumship. I had a rule that I never read for close friends or family, but she insisted, and eventually, I caved to her request and said I would read the Tarot cards for her. We began with her shuffling the pack, and my wife selected her cards. I laid them out in front of us and started to read. I explained what each card meant. On revealing the last card and following what had already been said, this card impacted me as I saw my marriage ending. At that moment, I heard the voice of my spirit friend gently informing me that 'this marriage will end soon.' No reason was given; it felt like someone had punched me in the chest. I was in love and determined to stay married. Not wanting to put that idea out there, I didn't tell Ann what I had heard. I just stopped reading and made a feeble excuse that I couldn't continue.

In total, the marriage had only lasted a year. In retrospect, we both knew that we were equally at fault, me because of my need to be wanted and loved, and Ann used the marriage to further her own needs in pursuing a career in which she believed being married was advantageous. Whilst I was away working, Ann packed and left the marital home. I only discovered this on my return. Sometime later, whilst I was away managing a pub as a stand-in, her solicitors found where I was working and unexpectedly served me with the divorce papers in the crowded bar. Stubbornly I was determined not to sign them. After all, I liked being married and still loved my wife. I went upstairs to my room. Sobbing, I became aware of the presence of Spirit and arms wrapping around me.

'I never wanted a divorce; I cried out.

Immediately the response came back.

'We know, but sign the papers; you don't know what is ahead for you.'

Angrily I said, 'what was the purpose of getting married in the first place if it had to end so soon?'

The reply came,

'Because she gave you structure and direction, which you needed.'

Not knowing what was meant by this statement, but knowing I could no longer swim against the tide, I signed the papers and returned them.

It was an amicable divorce.

After the marriage ended, I threw myself more and more into work; sometimes, I didn't leave the premises for months. Being the manager of licensed premises took up all my time. There was a growing awareness that I was missing out on things most people took for granted. I never watched television or frequented a cinema, and holidays were out of the question. Work consumed me. I believe that Spirit was becoming concerned at this turn of events as they started to make me aware that I had other skills yet unused. Maybe I should consider other careers away from catering as I was in danger of becoming a workaholic again.

On one of my rare days off, I found myself in the centre of Blackpool, standing outside the Job Centre. Once again, my spirit friend spoke to me, and I heard him telling me to go inside. Without hesitation, only trusting, I went inside and there right in front of me was an advert for a Civil Servant. All the other vacancies faded out of view. When I inquired about the position, the lady I asked informed me that she had just put the vacancy on the board as I walked in. Taking this as another sign and knowing this would afford me more free time, I applied for the job. After a call to the employer, I found myself sitting in front of a gentleman being interviewed the next day. He seemed to like me, even when I cheekily said I wanted his role within five years, and he offered me the post to start in the next month, subject to all the relevant security checks. I fitted in very well in this new role, and it suited my needs. I enjoyed working there and stayed for twelve years. For the first time in my life, I had a job where I didn't need to work evenings and weekends, but of course, I did, filling those hours working on Blackpool promenade in a café.

The extra free time meant I would regularly be more involved in the church and resume sitting with Elsie and the circle. I also started to socialise a little more, I never really felt comfortable in large social gatherings where alcohol was included and I never drank to excess due to the effects my mother's alcoholism had on me. I tried and tried again, but the thought of large groups of people drinking scared me.

Then there were the weekends at the now-famous Lindum Hotel that Glyn and Gordon were now running. It was good to catch up with the people I had now gotten to know and to be with spiritually like-minded folk again. I resumed my visits to Arthur Findlay college after my earlier hiatus. I loved to be around spiritual people and my enthusiasm for spirit communication remained. Stansted has been and will always be an influential part of my life.

On one memorable week there, run by Glyn, he asked me what I loved about my spiritual work. That wasn't hard. I pretty much loved everything about it and told him so. He then asked me what I didn't like about being a working medium. I said I didn't care much for one-to-one private readings. Still very shy, I felt awkward and unsure of myself when faced with a sitter. To which he replied, 'Mmmmm'. He returned to me later and said he had arranged one-to-one readings for me to do during the breaks and in the evenings. Knowing Glyn as I did, I knew there was a motive as yet unclear, so I complied with his request. The next day he asked if I now enjoyed doing them, to which I answered foolishly with an emphatic 'No'. Again, he lined up sitters for me to read during my breaks and evenings. After a few days and many readings later, when asked again and having learned my lesson, I responded enthusiastically and shouted 'Yes'.

I wanted to read for people who needed evidence of continuous life and the advice given by Spirit rather than what they wanted to hear or mere day-to-day concerns. I sent a thought out to Spirit asking that they bring such people to my attention. I was always amazed when this happened. One memorable night I decided to take a bus to meet some friends in Blackpool for an evening out. I was living in St Anne's at the time. Realising that I had just missed the bus because it had arrived early and the next one was not due for nearly half an hour, I decided to walk to the next stop to kill some time. While waiting, I heard the phone ringing from the telephone box on the other side of the road. The ringing was persistent; eventually, I crossed the road and answered it. At the end of the line was a woman who asked for me by name! I was stunned. She insisted that she needed to see me for a reading. I was shocked and confirmed that I was indeed the person she was looking for, and we made an appointment to meet up. It turned out the lady desperately required help with the grief she was struggling with. I do not believe in coincidences; I know I was meant to miss that bus. Such is the intelligence of Spirit that it does appear that heaven and earth can be moved, including buses, when the need arises.

My job in the civil service gave me much more freedom. I went to work early every day, which resulted in me building up a lot of flexitime. Still wanting that connection with Cumbria and the solace and healing the natural world gave me, I bought a pre-loved static caravan on a caravan park that people used for weekends away by the sea on the Solway Firth. The area was called Port Carlisle, 10 miles outside the city of Carlisle. It sat on the border between northwestern England and southwestern Scotland. I still needed solitude and the healing this place offered me so I would head there for weekends. I made a few new friends, and people would seek me out for a reading whenever I visited after discovering that I was a medium. Though I sometimes sought refuge from life, the spirit world would allow me this rest but always ensured that the people who needed spiritual solace would find me wherever I was.

Chapter 13

Letting Go

"To be delivered from the darkness, we first need to understand the light."

I saw my mother a little more often at this stage in my life. My sisters and I took care of her and her financial situation. In reality, our roles had reversed; we had become her parents. Although we didn't talk about the past, which was still painful for me, my mother needed me, so I was there for her. I did not use the past against her. I think it's a great shame that she did not know me, the man I had grown into. But I was content to continue this relationship and how it had become. Although she was only sixteen years my senior, her alcohol addiction resulted in her not ageing well. She had always been a beautiful woman, but as her looks faded, my mother withdrew from life, resulting in her neglecting her hygiene. It wasn't uncommon for us to remind her to shower and put on clean clothes we had laundered for her. Although we had a satisfactory relationship, I could still not tell her that I loved her because was no love for her in me, and she knew that. I accepted what she was and that this was her life, which was sad to watch.

My siblings and I shopped for our mother, ensuring

enough food in the house, although she ate very little. The drinking continued unabated, and she chain-smoked roll-ups. She lived alone, and one of my sisters and I thought having something in her life might benefit her. We got her a rescue dog, a Jack Russell. As it turned out, it was the right thing to do. She adored him. He was stone deaf and loved a cup of tea in the morning. He became her world, and she was devastated when he passed away some years later.

In December 2003, as Christmas approached, as usual, I wasn't looking forward to the festive period due in no small measure to the pain from my childhood. I knew it would be the usual round of picking up mum and one of my sisters and visiting the other sisters and their families. Such was my Christmas day, most of which I spent driving and then getting mum home before 6 pm as this was when she would start drinking. So, this year, I decided that I wanted it to be different, and I was determined not to feel guilty about doing something just for me. I was speaking to a friend about Christmas, and he, a single man too, said he was going to Lanzarote, one of the Canary Islands off the coast of West Africa, for the holiday period. It sounded like a great idea, so I asked if he minded me tagging along. He was happy, but I had to book my flights and accommodation.

I arranged to see my mother the week before Christmas before flying out. We did some shopping, and I took her to a café for something to eat. Although she ate very little, which wasn't uncommon, I couldn't help feeling something was off. She mentioned she was looking forward to spending Christmas with my sisters, as she knew one of their husbands would pick her up.

When it came time to leave, something felt different. I looked into my mother's eyes, they had always been the most beautiful blue, but now they seemed in some way to have dimmed. As I dropped her off at her home, she wished me a happy Christmas and said she hoped I would have a good holiday. I wished her the same, and I pulled away in my car. I looked back through the rear-view mirror, she gave me a little wave from the gate, and I knew this was goodbye. Something in me acknowledged that this was the last time I would see her, but I shook the feeling off and continued my journey home.

The much-anticipated day arrived, and I was off on holiday to Lanzarote. My friend had flown out an hour ahead of me as I couldn't get a ticket for the flight he was on. On arrival at the airport, he was waiting for me. We had separate apartments, which were lovely and a pool to chill out by. The weather was warm but windy, and we spent time exploring the area, discovering beautiful places to sit and eat or stop for a drink. I was feeling very relaxed. I had been there a few days, and my friend was off exploring when I realised something wasn't right. I had learned over the years to take notice of such feelings. Believing that my friend or I were in danger, I spoke to Spirit. I was reassured when they told me, 'It's not you, but ring home'. I found the nearest phone box and rang my sister to hear that our mother had died. One of my sisters had become concerned after getting no response from her on the phone. She went to mum's flat, broke in through a rear window, and discovered my mother had passed.

She was 56 years old.

I tried my very best but could not get back to the UK ahead of my flight scheduled two days later.

My sister Tracy phoned my maternal grandparents to inform them that their daughter had died. They had never really played a significant part in our lives and always seemed somewhat ambivalent towards us and now was no different.

'Well, I hope you aren't expecting us to pay for the funeral?' was the response from my grandfather when my sister finally got in touch with him.

That was not what we had expected. It upset us all. I was distraught and called my grandparents upon my return to the UK. I told them that we hadn't called looking for financial help and we were more than capable of meeting those costs. It was a courtesy call and nothing more. Their reaction did not surprise me. I recalled phoning them years ago when I had left home at 15, perhaps hoping they would take an interest in me as I felt I had no family. Their response then was,

'Well, what do you want us to do about it? We can't look after you'.

Every evening after work until her funeral, I visited the undertakers to sit with my mother. I talked about the things that had happened to me and the role that she had played. One evening as I sat and spoke to her, I expressed the profound pain that I had felt at her hand and how vulnerable I had been from all the abuse I had suffered from her and others. I could feel the little boy in me crying as I started to let my tears flow. This was the first time I had ever shown tears in her presence. As I gazed down at her for the final time, she looked peaceful, almost smiling, and I told her that I forgave her and hoped that she could carry on and work through her pain in her continuing life in the spirit realm. I placed five single-stem red roses representing her children and a letter I had written into the coffin. Then I asked the undertaker to seal the casket.

My mother was cremated, and her ashes interred in a churchyard in Lytham St Anne's. The night before the committal, on the way home from work, I called in at the funeral director's unannounced, fully expecting my mother's ashes to be inside the casket we had chosen. As the undertaker answered the door, I saw that he was flustered, and he started apologising. He ushered me into a private room where he picked up a supermarket carrier bag, placed it on the table, and apologised that he hadn't had time to put my mother's ashes in her casket. I reassured him that it was ok, and I found it highly amusing as it was very apt to her life.

The day of interment arrived. Torrential rain fell the

previous two days, and the ground was soggy underfoot. To reach my mother's final resting place, we followed the priest across a grassy area where my sister's high heels sunk as we walked to the far corner of the cemetery, much to their dismay and my amusement. The priest said some prayers and placed the casket containing our mother's ashes into the awaiting hole. Immediately it bobbed up and down and appeared to be moving about. The rain had saturated the ground and filled the void with water. My mother loved Rod Stewart, and I had chosen his song 'We are Sailing' for the accompanying music. As we watched, the casket looked for all the world as if it was sailing. I do believe that this was my mother having her final say. Some weeks later, I went to see the headstone we children had chosen and was assured had been erected. On arrival at her grave, I was shocked to find no headstone. At that moment, I heard my mother's voice say

'It's here, but you must look three spaces to the right.'

I did as she asked, and there it was. It was lovely as we had ordered, but the stonemason had neatly placed it on the wrong grave. Although shocked, I laughed simultaneously, recalling the adage that things come in threes. Indeed, this had been the case with my mother's remains. When I got home, I got in touch with the stonemasons and tried to start a dialogue with them about getting it moved. They were adamant that they had done everything correctly. I had no energy to deal with this, so my middle sister took over, and the next time I visited the grave, there was a new headstone. The one that had been wrongly placed was now sitting against the graveyard wall.

In the meantime, back at work, I was as busy as ever. On one of these days, we decided to have a meeting over lunch at the onsite restaurant. I ordered a jumbo sausage sandwich – something I could eat whilst working. I initially thought something wasn't right on tasting it, but this was superseded as the meeting was in full flow, and I thought nothing more of it as I ate. After work and at home, I ate a pork curry from the fridge for tea. In the middle of the night, I awoke feeling very unwell and began to vomit violently. My body seemed to want to eject everything from every available orifice. I have never felt so ill, and I recall crying out.

'Please, God help me.'

To which my spirit friend answered.

'You need to get to the hospital now!'

I know I was being helped as something took control, helping me dress, get in my car, and drive to the hospital two miles away. My only clear memory was standing at the accident and emergency department desk, and the receptionist asked me my name. I gave my name, and she continued asking me questions whilst I seemed to fade in and out of awareness. I heard myself say, 'excuse me', and I fell backwards. I listened to the receptionist shout for the triage nurse. The next thing I felt was flying through the air as I was picked up and placed on a bed. A doctor asked me if I had taken any drugs, to which I replied, 'I feel unwell' before becoming unconscious.

When I regained consciousness, I found myself in a busy room with several doctors and nurses moving urgently around my bed. I was calling out for Tina, my youngest sister, who worked as a nurse at the hospital. By chance, someone in the room knew her; the next thing I was aware of, she was standing over me. The doctors asked her if I was on drugs, to which she curtly replied, 'he's never taken drugs in his life.' They asked me what had happened, and I said I thought I had eaten something bad. My veins started collapsing, and they needed to get fluid into me. After several unsuccessful attempts, a surgeon was summoned to open a vein to insert a line. In the meantime, I asked my sister to get me a pill to make me get better so I could go home. With a concerned look, she told me in no uncertain terms that I wouldn't be going anywhere for the next few days.

Two male nurses were instructed to hold me down by my shoulders which panicked me. The doctor informed me that it was vital that fluids were rapidly introduced into my severely dehydrated body. This procedure, he went on to say, would be painful. And let me tell you, it was excruciatingly painful! I screamed as he squeezed the contents of two saline bags into my veins. Finally, I awoke on a ward with a couple of drips in my arms. I remained in the hospital for eight days until I could eat again. Throughout this ordeal, I felt the closeness of Spirit more profoundly than I had ever felt them. My Spirit team had been close to me the whole time, and I was acutely aware of how close to death I had been. I asked my Spirit friends, 'Why didn't I die?'

Then came the beautiful voice.

'Because you are loved and needed, and It wasn't your time.'

Chapter 14

Finding Home

"However far you move, you cannot escape the inevitable."

My mother's cat Bobby went missing after she had passed away. He was nowhere to be found, and I was worried about him wandering the streets. I contacted the RSPCA to see if anyone had handed in a cat that matched his description. Luckily, someone had, and so clutching a photograph of 'Bobby', I went along to see if he was the missing cat. As soon as I called his name, he came to me purring and meowing. I explained the circumstance that had caused the cat to be homeless, and a staff member gave me a choice to take him home or they would rehome him.

I was not a cat person. I nonetheless decided to take him because he was my mother's cat. He was a big tomcat; over time, 'Bobby' became known as 'Tom'. He settled well with me, and we lived happily together. Tom would accompany me on my weekends at the caravan in Cumbria. He became a welcome visitor, doing his rounds and visiting the other residents. He seemed to enjoy his weekends away and knew when it was time to return home. On one occasion, ignoring my increasingly desperate calls for him, I eventually found him snuggled into a hollow tree stump a few feet away, not happy that we had to leave.

I did what I did best and threw myself into work following my mother's passing. I met someone from London whose father lived in a small market town in the Cambridgeshire Fens, and one weekend we headed there for a visit. I felt at home in this semi-rural area and took off for a drive around to explore the area. Turning right, I found myself in a lovely little village. I stopped the car and took in my surroundings. As I looked to my right, I saw a bungalow to rent. I looked at it and liked where it stood; I loved everything about it and thought to myself.

"That's home."

When I inquired about it, I found that the gentleman we were visiting knew the people renting it out. On making enquiries from the people who owned the bungalow, they made a snap decision and were happy to rent it to me. I came away wondering what had just happened. With very little thought, I decided to move four hours across the country to the Southeast. I felt it was almost as if it was too easy, and things seemed to have been taken out of my hands. I was pretty happy with this, as Blackpool wasn't my home anymore. Although my sisters and friends were there, it had terrible memories and had taken a lot from me. Marie and Elsie would have loved me to stay, but they both understood that now was the time for me to move on.

Distance couldn't affect our friendship. I would phone them regularly and visit them on my frequent trips back to Blackpool.

I expected to move within three months as I had to sell my house. Things didn't go as smoothly as hoped. The people I was to rent the bungalow from were held up at their end by delays with building their new house. Eventually, my house sold, but my new home wasn't ready. I had an offer to go and stay in London for the interim, which I accepted. A few days before I left, I said my goodbyes to my sisters. There were no regrets as I handed over the keys to my house on the day of the move. I knew it was the right thing to do. Tom and I headed for London on the M6 motorway. We crossed over the Thelwall Viaduct, and I was looking forward to the new life ahead of me when I became aware of the presence of Spirit. I heard clearly, 'That is the last time you will see your baby sister.' This revelation threw me, my sister had previously tried to commit suicide, and I wondered if I should return. Perhaps there was something that I could do to prevent her death. Spirit responded with

"No, carry on". So, I did

It was a surreal moment. A feeling of peace descended on me, and there was no real focus on what was said. It seemed to melt away to a corner of my mind where it stayed, not unforgotten but not something I focused on. Therefore, it was no real surprise when I received a phone call four months later telling me that my sister had succeeded in taking her own life.

I went back to Blackpool to sort things out.

Her death was initially inconclusive, and my remaining three sisters tried to console themselves by refusing to believe she had taken her life. I knew she had because I had a visitation from her after her passing, and she accepted responsibility for ending her life. People often report following a bereavement that they have had a dream of their loved ones. These dreams or visitations are always very real, vivid, and easily remembered. I had such a visitation. My sister was there, talking to me and hugging me. Everything she ever had been, she still was. I awoke in tears; such was the emotion. I rang the sister I was closest to and told her, only to find out that she, too, had a similar visitation on the same night.

In some ways, my sister's death seemed to destroy something in me. It is a myth that mediums are unaffected by the passing of loved ones because they can connect to the Spirit world. Bereavement is a process we all must go through; the pain is no less when you are a medium. I began to drift. I stepped completely away from anything to do with mediumship at this time.

Eventually, the bungalow was ready, and I moved in. The village consisted of a predominantly elderly population. It was tranquil, and after about 7.30pm, nothing stirred apart from the odd tractor rumbling along the road. For once, I didn't hurl myself into work. I needed peace and a place to heal, and the vast gardens played a big part in that. They were unloved when I moved in, and I decided to commit my time to making them beautiful. Eventually, they became a paradise to me. Over time I noticed that a car would pull up outside and sit there. One day I saw the occupants getting a flask out and having a cup of tea. I asked if everything was okay as I had seen the two ladies sitting there on previous occasions. It turned out that they were mother and daughter who told me that they loved my garden so much they just came to admire it.

I believe Spirit guided me to get a dog one day quite out of the blue. Although I don't know this as a fact, I firmly believe it was to show me what unconditional love is. Tom was still with me. He loved living there. He was a contented cat, at liberty to roam the vast countryside and fields. I discovered that there were kennels just down the road from me. I made my way there and made enquiries about adopting. A lady showed me a couple of dogs that needed rehoming. I instantly fell in love with a little black and white dog found wandering in the area. He was a Japanese Chin, a breed I had never heard of until now. He was the same colour as Tom but much smaller. The kennels had to keep him for seven days, and only if his owner didn't claim him in that time could he be put up for adoption.

I asserted my interest in him, but my heart broke when his owner claimed him on the seventh day. Devastated, I asked Spirit why this dog was shown to me when it would never be mine. As I sat there wondering, I noticed an advert on my computer from a particular dog breeder looking to rehome one of her ex-show dogs, and it was a Japanese Chin. I knew that advert was Spirit in action. Not for the first time in my life, they had given me a sign. This particular breed was rare in Britain then, yet here was an advert for one. I inquired about the dog and made an appointment to go and see it the following week. My sister came to stay with me and accompanied me to see the dog. The day before we went, I told her I would be returning with two dogs, not one. Looking at me quizzically, she asked, 'how do you know that? To which I replied,' I just know.'

Upon arrival, the breeder showed us a fourteen-month-old female dog who had given birth to one puppy. The little dog was so lively and full of character. I loved her instantly. Many dogs were running around. Sitting alone and being pushed around by the others was a small female in the corner. The breeder said she was looking to rehome her as she was picked on a lot. She was a little over two and a half years old and had had two litters. The breeder said I could take her if I promised to have her spayed. I didn't have the heart to say no, and said,

"Well, it looks like she's coming home with us."

I turned to my sister and said,

'Two dogs',

She just raised her eyebrows.

And so, I came home with Poppy and Kiki, both Japanese Chins. They got on well with Tom, who enjoyed hiding behind the pot plants, ambushing Poppy, and making her jump. Life seemed settled for us until one day, the landlord decided to build a house in the field to the side of my bungalow, meaning the new place would spoil my view of the surrounding countryside. I asked if I could move into the new property once it was built and was given the assurance that I could. After its completion, the dogs, myself and Tom moved into our new home.

Kiki, Poppy & Percy

A few months after the move next door, Tom, who was getting old, fell ill. Sadly, he had to be put to sleep. He was the last connection I had to my mother. Within that month of his passing, Kiki and Poppy's breeder phoned me and asked if I would take an ex-show dog who was Poppy's son. She wanted him to be with his mum. Of course, I said yes. People often say that dogs don't recognise their offspring. I beg to differ. I bought Percy home. Kiki eyed him suspiciously, not knowing what to make of this new family member. As soon as Poppy saw him, she ran towards him and started licking his face, and he, in return, was licking hers. They did this for over ten minutes. Her tail never stopped wagging, and I had never seen her so animated. There was no doubt that they recognised one another. Eventually, all three dogs settled in very well together.

Chapter 15

Who Am I?

"Place your hand in my hand, and I will stand with you."

I had no idea where my life was going, but somehow, I knew I was where I was supposed to be. The sadness of my baby sister's passing was a heavy blanket I wore, and this dark period in my life was one in which I merely existed. I let things go on around me that I wouldn't have ordinarily.

The gardens in my new home closely resembled a building site. Alone with my dogs but buoyed by the interest of the two ladies who had sat outside the bungalow drinking tea, I set about creating two new gardens. As they developed over time, they drew approving looks from passers-by who would stop and chat, and one day a lady from the village approached me. We talked about the design and layout, and she asked many questions about the plants I used. After a while, she informed me that she was the organiser of an Open Garden event to help raise money for charity and asked if I would give visitors access to my garden on specific weekends. Pleased with her comments, I happily agreed. Loving nature and gardening, I had an idea to make myself a modest income that would pay for the ongoing plans I had for my garden. I bought some plants from a plant auction and began selling them outside my house. People would stop to look at my work in the garden and buy plants.

Two ladies, one of whom would become a lifelong friend, came and bought most of the plants before asking me if I would consider doing their gardens for them. I would have carte blanche to design and plant how I saw fit. Never having considered this as a direction I might take in life, this opportunity had seemingly fallen into my lap. I readily agreed, and what would become a short career as a gardener started. Word spread throughout the area, and my reputation grew. Before long, I became swamped with work, and my garden was being neglected.

I frequented the village pub for meals and became friendly with the landlord and landlady, who heard of my reputation as a gardener. They asked me to take on their garden. Over time they discovered I had previous experience cheffing and running pubs. Their last chef had left without notice and had no success replacing him, meaning their business's food side was failing. I offered advice on organisation and how to make their restaurant profitable again. One thing led to another, and eventually, my gardening enterprise ended, and I went back to cheffing at the pub. It suited me well, the pub was only down the road, and I did lunchtimes and evenings for them. We did roasts that became very popular in the area. Sundays were always fully booked throughout the day. Cheffing wasn't something I had planned to pursue anymore. I thought I had left it behind when I moved away from Blackpool. Life experience told me there was a reason for me to be there at that time, so I stuck with it.

One day, the subject turned to spiritual matters during a conversation with the landlady. I mentioned I could see a gentleman and pointed out to her where he was sitting in the bar. She responded that the man I was describing was dead and where I had pointed to was where he used to sit. I told her about two other people I could see, and she again confirmed that they were 'dead'. The landlady was very interested in all things of this nature, and when I gave her details about her deceased aunt, she was completely floored. As with most villages, word travels fast, and it soon got around the area that I had this gift, and people would approach me asking for readings. One woman was interested in me and wanted to start a home circle. She came to me looking for advice, and eventually, I trained her to become a circle leader, of which I became a member.

In the meantime, one of my sisters had come to visit. We were in the garden weeding the borders and chatting about nothing in particular when she looked up, smiled at me and asked if she could say something, to which I, of course, said yes. Quite psychic herself, she said,

'Since I've been here, I've been watching you. You are alive, but I can see you are not living as I look into your eyes. I see life, but I don't see you.'

It felt like someone had kicked me in the chest as she

said that, and I knew what she meant. I knew that Spirit had instigated her words to wake me up and bring me back to life. I burst into tears. Sobbing deeply for what seemed like forever, I couldn't stop. The years of abuse, my baby sister taking her own life, the lack of love, loss, grief, and much more came tumbling out. I had only ever cried like that once before. It was with Marie. My sister held me for a while before going and making a cup of coffee. Together we sat there looking at the garden, the beautiful blue sky and the nature surrounding us. Finally, she turned to me and spoke.

"Now, doesn't that feel better?"

And, of course, it did. I doubt that my sister realised what her words had done for me. It was a cathartic moment as I let a lifetime of tears go, and now, on reflection, I know this was the first step to a new life.

I continued working at the pub and doing occasional readings for those who wanted them. I attended the circle the lady had started and made a few friends. But there were problems within the group. Knowing this was the first circle the leader had run, I offered her suggestions that she often treated with disdain, and there were times I felt she belittled me. On one occasion, I offered her some advice contrary to her teaching during circle, and she was unhappy about that. A couple of days later, she invited me to join her at a café for coffee, and I knew she wanted to discuss my 'interference'. She berated me, saying that she was in charge and had to have control, and the circle members were confused as to who was running it. I apologised, of course. But unbeknown to her, some circle members had been coming to me looking for advice. I always tried to help them but ultimately directed them back to the circle leader as protocol dictated.

After this scolding, I asked Spirit for advice.

"You've got to answer me now," I said

"I don't need this. How I am being treated is wrong. Tell me if there is a purpose in staying because I'm happy to leave it here and now."

Spirit responded in no uncertain terms,

"You need to stay and put up with it for a while longer."

I knew not to ignore what Spirit advised me; I trusted them, so I stayed. I put up with the belittling and did not react to her attempts to embarrass me. She organised days where people came for readings for a fee from the members of our circle. Instead of paying the mediums, she kept the money for the 'running of the circle,' she said. I didn't comment on this. I knew I was there for a purpose, although Spirit hadn't yet revealed what that actually was. At their behest, I continued attending the circle and talked more to my spirit guide at home. I loved sitting in the stillness and peace. On one occasion, as I sat sending out my thoughts to the Spirit world, I said

"I know you want me here, but why? I understand that there has been a plan here, and although I thought I had drifted, which I may have, I realise now that you were the current in which I was drifting."

The voice said,

"You needed to find your voice, your peace and who you are".

Little by little, life started to feel brighter. I loved my home, and I was delighted with my dogs. I had a few dear friends, and I never felt the need for anything more. Through a friend from the circle, I learned about a Mind, Body and Spirit (M.B.S.) event that she was attending. Before I thought about it, I heard myself asking if I could get a place there to do readings. After some form filling, I was invited to be a reader, and in 2012 I did my first event. It was successful, and I gave readings at similar events resulting in me getting a name for myself on that circuit. I began occasionally serving local Spiritualist churches while asking Spirit if I should continue attending the circle because my situation there was becoming untenable. It wasn't pleasant, and I knew that the circle leader wasn't doing things correctly. Working at the pub was no longer the pleasure it once was. The landlady had developed a brain aneurysm that made her behaviour unpredictable and volatile. Working for her became hugely difficult. In the end, I had to leave. It was sad because the landlord begged me to reconsider, but I was adamant.

One evening when life seemed to become too much, I spoke to my spirit guide, my past was now haunting me, and I couldn't quite see my worth. I was examining my past relationships, and I felt that they had been about what I could give them, and at that moment, I felt incredibly lonely. I began to cry. Through the tears, I knew the real reason I was crying. It wasn't the job, circle, or position I now found myself in. It was because I felt unloved.

I almost shouted to Spirit.

"Why can't I just be loved for me? Why can I not feel true love?"

Looking back at my life, I didn't know what love was other than that of my dogs.

I demanded that Spirit give me an answer, telling them I couldn't carry on the way I was and wanted to feel and share real love. I finished by saying,

"This cannot be my life".

I heard my guide Matthew clearly in the room I sat in, gently reassuring me that I did deserve to be loved.

I responded by asking if I would ever meet somebody. To which Matthew replied,

"Yes, you will."

Encouraged by his response, I asked what this person would be like and if he could describe her to me.

"She's 5ft 2inches, brunette, she's a lovely person, who has a personality to match yours."

Feeling euphoric and brave, I decided to push the boat

out, knowing that Spirit usually would not give me the information I was about to ask for, but I said,

"Will you give me a name?"

Much to my surprise, I heard.

"Yes, her name is Sarah."

Emboldened by this, I decided to push a little further.

'When will we meet?' I persisted.

"Ah" (my heart sank), "she is neither ready nor are you. Can you answer this – you say you want someone who can love you just for you?"

"Yes", I answered

"How can you expect someone to love you for you when you don't love yourself? It makes me weep."

I felt as though someone had driven a dagger into my heart.

"What do I need to do?" I asked.

"You know what you need to do. I'm always here to help you."

Chapter 16

Sarah

"I sought salvation, and salvation sought me."

The realisation was clear. I knew I had to work on myself. So began a period of intense reflection as I revisited the abuse I had suffered. It was acutely painful, but I had to find peace. I had blamed myself for my mother's cruelty for too long, believing she couldn't love me because I had been born too soon. I looked at what I was doing, how I reacted instead of acting, why I was terrified of things, my shyness, and my mistrust of people. It took a long time to come to terms with everything. I wasn't successful all the time, it took a couple of years, but I worked hard on myself.

Time passed, and I was still sitting in the circle and putting up with the leader's tedious antics, and one night a new group of people joined us for a spiritual Christmas party. I found myself sitting with three ladies I had never met before. I was tasked with giving a reading to the young woman sitting next to me, and she took the information that I brought forward. I noticed that she smiled a lot and played with her hair when I heard my guide say,

'That's Sarah'.

I responded, "I know. She told me who she was when she introduced herself".

Again, the voice

"That's Sarah"

It had been nearly three years since my conversation with Spirit about someone coming into my life.

I felt like someone had elbowed me in the ribs. I jumped as I heard,

'That's THE Sarah!'.

I turned and looked at the girl sitting next to me, and in that moment of realisation, I was stunned. I saw her for the first time. I realised she was how Spirit described her all those years before. I was attracted to her, but my shyness overwhelmed me, and I did not pursue her after our initial meeting. Our destiny needed some help from Spirit, and some weeks later, I woke up feeling compelled to go and visit a particular garden centre some miles away.

While looking around the centre, I heard my guide telling me to go and visit my friend Heather who lived close by. I decided I would have lunch first, but the voice of my guide insisted that I go immediately. Thinking something was amiss and perhaps Heather was in trouble, I headed to her house. I knocked on the door, and she answered. Her face showed surprise that I was there, but she invited me inside. As I entered the lounge, I saw Sarah seated in a chair and realised why Spirit had directed me there. I discovered that Sarah had gone to see Heather and asked questions about me. Heather apologised and said she had a couple of readings to do, so we would have to leave.

I looked at Sarah and said, 'Come on, let's go for a coffee.' Usually, I wouldn't have been so forward, but everything seemed right. My shyness dissolved. We went for a coffee and the whole day sped by as we chatted. Sarah told me that she had been trying to attract my attention that evening we first met. Her partner had not long passed from cancer. She attended several Spiritualist church services following his passing and was told she would meet someone within six months. Twice, she dismissed the idea as she neither wanted that nor was ready for it. At a third church, when told the same by the medium, she knew it would happen, and she accepted with the proviso that she was only interested if he had dogs and could cook.

I fit that requirement exactly, plus I was a medium, a subject Sarah was deeply interested in. I saw now why the dogs had come into my life. We got on well and talked about everything. We had lots in common and spent more and more time together as we quickly fell in love. I soon realised that I couldn't imagine my life without her. By now, I had returned briefly to the cheffing job in the village after the landlord approached me needing help. His wife had left him by now, and I felt I could work there again.

That year for my birthday, Sarah and I went to a restaurant with some friends; I had decided that I wanted to marry her. I had told her on the day I met her at Heather's house that we would marry one day, to which she had smiled. On the night of my birthday, armed with an engagement ring, I thanked everyone for the gifts they had given me and told them that there was one present I would love to have, which was missing. Turning to Sarah, I pulled out the engagement ring and asked her to marry me. It seemed as if time stood still as she sat there looking at me with her mouth open until a friend said,

'Well, are you going to answer?'

Luckily for me, she said yes.

Things happened so fast, but I knew it was the right thing. I could feel the happiness of Spirit. Sarah has played a massive part in my self-healing. Through her, I found my self-worth. I became stronger and understood why I had to stay in that circle. It was so that I could meet her. When she realised how unhappy I was there, she gave me the strength to walk away, and it wasn't long before I left an unpleasant situation behind me and moved on.

Sarah and I were inseparable as our lives blossomed in the following months. I now knew what true love was. We discussed where we would live as the village I lived in was too far for Sarah to commute daily, and we decided to move closer to her job. One morning having coffee, Sarah was looking at houses online, and without really looking, I jokingly pointed at a place and said, "that's the one". Sarah booked a viewing and liked it but couldn't commit until I had seen it. I felt a sense of urgency, and I knew I just had to see it as soon as possible and arranged the earliest appointment the next day. The landlady was in attendance with the estate agent, and she expressed that she liked us and would like us to be her tenants. We made plans to move which meant giving up my cheffing job. With Sarah's support, we decided that now was the time to begin working professionally as a medium.

Around this time, my middle sister, a breast cancer survivor, began experiencing pain in her shoulder. She had emigrated to New Zealand with her partner and her daughter after winning the initial battle with cancer. Now the doctors there told her that it had returned and was aggressive. She moved back to England to be near family and friends. I pleaded with Spirit to give her more time. I asked for eight years, and the response was,

"She's had eight years."

Which was correct, including the first time she had the disease.

During this time, I commuted between home and Blackpool to be with her, and three weeks before her passing, she was in Blackpool hospital. My sister knew about my mediumship but never really believed in it. As I was sitting with her one day, she turned to me and spoke.

'Can I tell you something? I believe now.'

'Believe what?' I replied.

'In what you do'.

'Why is that?'

'Because I have seen mum and our sister. They have visited me.'

'What did they say?' I asked.

'They told me everything was going to be fine.'

I knew, of course, what it meant. That her time was coming and that it would be soon. It isn't unusual for those close to passing to be visited by loved ones that have crossed over. That helped me, and I asked her if we could have a 'password' that she would use to connect with me. She agreed, and we decided on one. Despite contacting me several times since passing, she has yet to use this word.

A couple of weeks later, Sarah and I were eating in a restaurant when I got a phone call telling me my sister's condition had worsened, and if I wanted to see her, I should go now. We dropped everything and raced to Blackpool. Her passing was peaceful, even beautiful. After sitting with her for hours, I was aware of the shift in energy in the room. She just drifted into unconsciousness before her heart stopped some hours later. So often, people believe that our endings will be dramatic and upsetting like we see in films, but there was none of that. I watched her body's process as it shut down and the serenity on her face as she slipped away. Finally, her Spirit was free. Her death was so different from that of my younger baby sister. With this passing, we were blessed with an opportunity to say goodbye. Sarah was an incredible support to myself and my family during this difficult time.

After my sister's passing, Sarah and I finally moved into our new home in which we currently live. It is in a rural village near Peterborough - the city I had visited years before on my initial visit to Stansted. We married a few months later, and I felt my sister's presence with us on the day. I had found love with Sarah. This sassy, strong lady who knows her own mind has helped me on so many levels and has been instrumental in me taking my mediumship forward professionally.

Chapter 17

An Ordinary Life

"The Seeds of Hope will Flourish Even amongst the Gravel"

After Sarah and I moved into our house, we decided to make it into our home and concentrated on making it look lovely. No mean feat as, alongside this, we were finalising our wedding while I was still reeling from my sister's passing to cancer. I didn't withdraw from life or go into myself, unlike before. The loving support I received from Sarah and being with my sister ahead of her passing helped me through the grief.

With all of this taking place, Sarah and I decided it was the right time for me to take a leap of faith and work professionally as a medium. I checked this with my spirit friends and was told to 'have faith,' but I have to admit I was terrified by this prospect. It took courage to stop earning a regular income from an employer. Sarah and I set about designing and constructing a website to advertise my work. My spirit team kept telling me it would be fine, that everything would work out and that I needed to trust my guides. Reassuring because I continued to doubt whether I was good enough. I needn't have worried as I hit the ground running. I always strive to do my best for

Spirit and my clients. All mediums, even those with many years of experience, will occasionally doubt themselves due to wanting to be true to themselves and Spirit. Glyn's voice rang in my ears when I doubted myself, telling me I was a good medium and needed to remember his words.

My name got around the local churches, and they invited me to take their services, which grew to include many others around the country. Church services remain something I enjoy, as I feel I'm giving back to the spirit world. Word has spread, and the website's help has brought people to me who needed the reassurance that life goes on. I continued working at Mind Body Spirit events for a while, where Sarah joined me. Whilst I gave readings, she manned a small stall selling spirit-related gifts. I continued to sit for trance at home with Sarah, and as always, the wisdom from the Spirit world never failed to inspire us.

Life is joyous, but it's not all about laughter, and like so many others, we have experienced the loss of family members. We were due to go to Germany the Christmas after our wedding to see Sarah's family. Sadly, Sarah's mother unexpectedly passed away before we could get there, which was a massive shock followed a few years later by the sad passing of Sarah's father. Early 2020 saw the beginnings of the devastating pandemic that would affect us all. During the first lockdown, my father took his transition to Spirit with a condition unrelated to Covid. We were fortunate to attend a small funeral that marked his life despite restrictions. After Sarah and I had married, I had become a little closer to him, and we would share our mutual love of birdwatching and gardening. I looked past his childishness and could communicate with him as a son ought to.

In 2021 my sister, a year younger than me, became very unwell. We talked on the phone, and I spoke to her just before Christmas when the voices again told me that she was not long for this world, and I voiced this to Sarah. Some would say being a medium isn't a gift in these circumstances, but I believe Spirit was preparing me as it is through loss that we learn some of our hardest lessons. I am no different from anyone else except that I know that we never really lose anyone forever. When the time comes to shed our mortal coil, we are reunited with those for whom we grieve. And so, it was two months later; my sister passed over.

Sarah has bolstered me throughout these sad times, and her support has been invaluable. A great sadness to us both was the loss of our doggy family as they grew older and left us to take their place in the Spirit World. They were our children, and I know we will see them again. Although we have no dogs now, a local stray cat has adopted us and is a daily visitor. We are happy because we are content with what we have. We are not money rich, but there has always been enough for our needs and a comfortable life.

The pandemic resulted in churches closing temporarily, but the rise of Zoom has meant I could take virtual services and continue my readings. Sarah was furloughed through the first lockdown as I took my work online. Together we took the opportunity to update the house. I know this was a stressful period for some, taking a toll on their relationships. Ours seemed to get stronger. I realised that this beautiful lady was not just my wife but indeed my best friend. Reflecting on my life, I acknowledge that I am blessed in many ways.

The river of life has brought me to a place and time that is right and perfect for me, with the right person. Sometimes, it seemed that I had drifted through life (or had I?). I knew I didn't fight the flow; I had allowed Spirit to guide me where I needed to be. Had I resisted, my life could have been very different. I love what I'm doing and can't see that changing.

Life is about learning, and I am no different in this. I continue to develop my mediumship skills through many avenues, including the SNU (Spiritualist National Union). Alongside readings, I now mentor those wishing to develop their mediumship. As I write this, I recall the faces of those I learned many lessons from. I often hear myself repeating their wise words to my students. Coincidently (or is it?), a village hall stands next door to our house, which I now use for my many teaching events. Wanting to be of continuous service to Spirit, I have attained my Certificate of accreditation from the SNU, and I continue to further my learning through many avenues of training. Although I have over thirty years of experience, I believe that we should strive to keep learning. Because mediumship is so important to me, I do not think I can sit back and say I have reached a point where I know everything. As a teacher, I believe I owe this to my students.

So dear reader, we've taken this journey through my life together. I am an average man, leading an everyday life, earning a living in a less-than-ordinary way. You may wonder how I can say I'm an average man when looking at my life and what has happened to me. That would be understandable, but Spirit has always been a part of my life. I have nothing to measure it against. It has been ordinary but has contained some extraordinary events. Through the love of those from the unseen world who have guided me through those events that I might not have ordinarily survived, I now understand how blessed I am. They have loved, protected, and cherished me. I am by no means any different to you. But I have not become a victim through the love of God and Spirit. Although realising this has taken me a lifetime, I'm here! If my experience has taught me anything, I know you, too, are loved by that divine presence and can meet the challenges set before you if only you believe you are loved, worth loving, and have a voice.

As I come to the close of this book, sitting here now, I hear the voices from my past. Elsie, my circle mother. Marie, my angel mother. Glyn, my friend and mentor, and Gordon, who I had aspired to be like. I do not forget Betty, who encouraged my progress despite my fear of her. Teachers, all who became dear friends, I know that they have not gone. Nor are they in the past. They are very much here in the present. They live on not only in me but in my work and the world around us. Their love still touches my heart, their wisdom still impacts my mind, and I owe them a debt of gratitude I doubt I could ever repay. I hope I have done them justice by including them in this book. I have never regretted becoming a professional medium, and my only desire is to bring proof that life does continue so that people can live their best lives. I often wonder if the messages I give change people's lives. I will never truly know, but then someone will tell me that a reading they had with me has given them the evidence they needed, bringing them hope and the ability to carry on. Spirit cannot tell us what to do, but the messages they bring often lift us enough to allow us to take the next step.

I thank God I have been a tiny part of this endeavour.

Chris Jacobs CSNU is an acclaimed British Medium, Tutor and Author.

Chris offers worldwide private readings via Zoom, Skype and Messenger. He is an experienced tutor and holds regular workshops as well as Mediumship Mentorship Programmes in person and online. Chris regularly demonstrates at Spiritualist Churches, Centres and public venues.

For further information about Chris Jacobs work, please visit his website:

www.chrisjacobsmedium.co.uk

Further Reading

Gordon Higginson - On the Side of Angels

Anthony Borgia -The world Unseen

Arthur Findlay – On the Edge of the Etheric & The Unfolding Universe

Tony Stockwell - Walking with Angels

Glyn Edwards – The Spirit World in Plain English,

Spirit Gems: Essential Guidance for Spiritual, Mediumistic and Creative Unfoldment

Teachings from Silver Birch (Silver Birch Series)

Stewart Alexander – An Extraordinary Journey: The memoirs of a Physical Medium

A Life Far From Ordinary

Printed in Great Britain
by Amazon

87571745R00095